The Jewish

Also by Daniel Boyarin

Intertextuality and the Reading of Midrash

Carnal Israel: Reading Sex in Talmudic Culture

A Radical Jew: Paul and the Politics of Identity

*Unheroic Conduct: The Rise of Heterosexuality and the
Invention of the Jewish Man*

*Dying for God: Martyrdom and the Making of Christianity
and Judaism*

Queer Theory and the Jewish Question

Border Lines: The Partition of Judaeo-Christianity

Socrates and the Fat Rabbis

The Jewish Gospels

The Story of the Jewish Christ

Daniel Boyarin

Requests for permission to reproduce selections from this book should be made
through our website: https://thenewpress.com/contact.

Originally published in the United States by The New Press, New York, 2012
This paperback edition published by The New Press, 2013
Distributed by Two Rivers Distribution

ISBN 978-1-59558-878-4 (pbk.)
ISBN 978-1-59558-711-4 (ebook)

LIBRARY OF CONGRESS CATALOGING-IN-PUBLICATION DATA
Boyarin, Daniel.
The Jewish Gospels : the story of the Jewish Christ / Daniel Boyarin.
p. cm.
Includes bibliographical references and index.
ISBN 978-1-59558-468-7 (hc. : alk. paper)
1. Jesus Christ—Jewish interpretations. 2. Bible. N.T.—
Criticism, interpretation, etc., Jewish. I . Title.
BM620.B69   2011
296.3'96—dc23   2011034643

The New Press publishes books that promote and enrich public discussion
and understanding of the issues vital to our democracy and to a more equitable world.
These books are made possible by the enthusiasm of our readers; the support of a
committed group of donors, large and small; the collaboration of our many partners
in the independent media and the not-for-profit sector; booksellers, who often
hand-sell New Press books; librarians; and above all by our authors.

www.thenewpress.com

Composition by dix!
This book was set in Berling Lt Std

Printed in the United States of America

For Aharon Shemesh, נ״י,
in whom I have fulfilled both directives of our Sages:
to find a friend and acquire a teacher

Contents

Foreword

Jack Miles

"DANIEL BOYARIN," A PROMINENT CONSERVATIVE rabbi confided to me not long ago, "is one of the two or three greatest rabbinic scholars in the world," and—dropping his voice a notch—"possibly even the greatest." The observation was given in confidence because, quite clearly, it troubled the rabbi to think that someone with Boyarin's views might have truly learned Talmudic grounds for them. As a Christian, let me confide that his views can be equally troubling for Christians who appreciate the equally grounded originality of his reading of our New Testament.

Boyarin's is a troubling brilliance because it blurs and complicates a pair of reciprocally settled identities. His achievement is to have taken conceptual control of this reciprocity and then deployed it in a bold rereading of the rabbis and the evangelists alike, the results of which are so startling that once you—you, Jew, or you, Christian—get what he is up to, you suddenly read even the most familiar passages of your home scripture in a new light.

I can best illustrate this point, I think, with a recent,

quite personal example, but let me first set the scene with a little parable exploring what I mean by "reciprocally settled identities." There is in our neighborhood a family with twin sons, Benjamin and Joshua. Because they are fraternal twins, not identical, they don't look alike, and they are different in other ways as well. Ben is an athlete, a scrappy competitor who makes up in hustle whatever he may lack in raw ability. Josh is a singer-songwriter with bedroom eyes whose second love, after his current girl-friend, is his guitar. Their mother, who comes from a fam-ily of athletes, says fondly of Ben, "He's all boy, that one." Their father, from a family of musicians and romantics, dotes on Josh.

Being twins, sharing a bedroom since they were tod-dlers, Ben and Josh know one another quite well. Ben knows—as no one else does—that Josh can beat him in one-on-one basketball. Josh knows that Ben can sing two-part harmony in a sweet tenor voice never heard outside their bedroom. But what they know about them-selves has mattered less and less as time has passed and as a received version of who they are has taken hold in their extended family. Ben is the athlete and fighter, ev-eryone in the family agrees; Josh is the singer and lover, and that's that. By degrees, the brothers themselves have succumbed to the family definition. Ben has virtually for-gotten that he, too, can sing. Josh has stopped working out and this year did not even go to the homecoming game.

Reciprocally, but with family assistance, they have accepted simplified versions of themselves as their settled identities.

As it happens, though, the twins have a favorite teacher, Mr. Boyarin, who knows them both from school and once accepted an invitation to Thanksgiving dinner at their house. After dinner, as sometimes happens on such occasions, the family album was brought out for the visitor's edification. Mr. Boyarin, who likes both boys, noticed a fifth-grade photo of Josh—Josh, not Ben—in football equipment and asked about it. Later, he noticed a photo of Ben—Ben, not Josh—singing the national anthem at the school convocation, chosen for the honor because Mrs. Pignatelli, the music teacher, knew a great boy soprano when she heard one. The family chuckled at these completely out-of-character moments, but Mr. Boyarin took quiet note and resolved, as the opportunity may present itself, to allow what he sees as the neglected if not entirely suppressed side of each boy a little room to operate in.

Daniel Boyarin sees Judaism and Christianity as being like Josh and Ben, not that either sports or music is at issue. At issue, rather, is the question—always consequential but perhaps never more so than after the destruction of the Jewish Temple in 70 C.E.—of how Jews should relate to their God and to the Gentile majority of the human race. Before the destruction of the Temple, there were various contending schools of thought about this core question.

After the catastrophic destruction, the two schools that survived were the Rabbinical and the Christian. Theologically, they had their differences, but they were both Jewish as surely as Josh and Ben are both brothers in the same family. Their differences were, as we say, all in the family, and they remained all in the family not just for a few decades but, Boyarin boldly asserts, for the first few centuries of the common era. It took that long for gradually escalating mutual polemics to overcome an underlying sense of fraternity on either side and to create two reciprocally settled identities where before there had been just one identity, albeit unsettled. What Boyarin regrets is that these two identities were polemically simplified and coarsened as each side learned to repudiate, as if on deepest principle, practices and beliefs that, at an earlier stage, either side would have admitted as unproblematically its own. It is as if Ben's great-grandchildren should be taught to believe as a matter of core identity that "we never touch the guitar, *they* play the guitar, that's what they're like," while Josh's offspring, by the same token, should be taught to stake their lives on the self-evident truth that "we never touch a football, *they* play football, that's what they're like."

Did Jesus keep kosher? Would that have been un-Christian of him? In chapter 3 of the book you are about to read, titled "Jesus Kept Kosher," Boyarin writes:

Most (if not all) of the ideas and practices of the Jesus movement of the first century and the beginning of the second century—and even later—can be safely understood as part of the ideas and practices that we understand to be "Judaism.". . . The ideas of Trinity and incarnation, or certainly the germs of those ideas, were already present among Jewish believers well before Jesus came on the scene to incarnate in himself, as it were, those theological notions and take up his messianic calling.

However, the Jewish background of the ideas of the Jesus movement are only one piece of the new picture I'm sketching here. Much of the most compelling evidence for the Jewishness of the early Jesus communities comes from the Gospels themselves. . . . Counter to most views of the matter, according to the Gospel of Mark, Jesus kept kosher, which is to say that he saw himself not as abrogating the Torah but as defending it. There was controversy with some other Jewish leaders as to how best to observe the Law, but none, I will argue, about *whether* to observe it. According to Mark (and Matthew even more so), far from abandoning the laws and practices of the Torah, Jesus was a staunch defender of the Torah against what he perceived to be threats to it from the Pharisees.

The Pharisees were a kind of reform movement within the Jewish people that was centered on Jerusalem and Judaea. The Pharisees sought to convert

other Jews to their way of thinking about God and
Torah, a way of thinking that incorporated seeming
changes in the written Torah's practices that were
mandated by what the Pharisees called "the tradition of the Elders.". . . It is quite plausible, therefore,
that other Jews, such as the Galilean Jesus, would
reject angrily such ideas as an affront to the Torah
and as sacrilege.

Boyarin's reading of Mark 7, in which he turns what
Christianity has traditionally interpreted as an attack on
Jewish dietary and purity laws into a distinct kind of defense of them, is one of many stunningly persuasive but
utterly surprising readings of what in his hands does indeed become "compelling evidence for the Jewishness of
the early Jesus communities . . . from the Gospels themselves." There is no denying, and Boyarin does not deny,
that Jesus attacks the Pharisees, the forerunners if not the
founders of Rabbinical Judaism, but few Christian commentators have recognized how clear a distinction Jesus
draws between them and Moses and how much he is at
pains to defend Moses and therewith to defend the Torah.
It is by stressing that distinction that Boyarin brings the
quarrel back into the Jewish family.

Now to the personal example. On October 30, 2011,
I heard the following Gospel passage read in my church
(Church of the Messiah, Santa Ana, California):

Jesus said to the crowds and to his disciples, "The scribes and the Pharisees sit on Moses' seat; therefore, do whatever they teach you and follow it; but do not do as they do, for they do not practice what they teach. They tie up heavy burdens, hard to bear, and lay them on the shoulders of others; but they themselves are unwilling to lift a finger to move them. They do all their deeds to be seen by others; for they make their phylacteries broad and their fringes long. They love to have the place of honor at banquets and the best seats in the synagogues, and to be greeted with respect in the marketplaces, and to have people call them rabbi. But you are not to be called rabbi, for you have one teacher, and you are all students. And call no one your father on earth, for you have one Father—the one in heaven. Nor are you to be called instructors, for you have one instructor, the Messiah. The greatest among you will be your servant. All who exalt themselves will be humbled, and all who humble themselves will be exalted. (Matthew 23:1–12; New Revised Standard Version)

Jesus was surely one of the greatest polemicists of all time. It is thanks to him that the very word "Pharisee" has as its second definition in *Webster's College Dictionary* "a sanctimonious, self-righteous, or hypocritical person." And it's clear, isn't it, in this passage from the Gospel of

Matthew that the sanctimonious, self-righteous, hypo-critical persons whom Jesus has in his crosshairs do call one another "rabbi." But all texts, including scripture, are read through the filter of what one "already knows." Episcopalians who call their priests "Father" and Roman Catholics who call the pope "Holy Father" slide easily enough past "call no one your father on earth, for you have one Father—the one in heaven" because "everyone knows" that the term *father* is innocently used in these Christian contexts. More to the point, most Christian interpreters slide with equal ease past Jesus' injunction: "The scribes and the Pharisees sit on Moses's seat; therefore, *do whatever they teach you and follow it.*" I myself have read and heard this passage for years but only on October 30, 2011, thinking about my draft of this foreword, did I really lock on to *do whatever they teach you and follow it*. Post-Boyarin, I can only read this passage as a *defense* of un-sanctimonious, un-self-righteousness, un-hypocritical adherence to the Law of Moses against sanctimonious, self-righteous, hypocritical exploitation of it.

So, then, I repeat the question: did Jesus keep kosher? If he had nothing against the Law, why couldn't he keep kosher? And come to think of it, is it not a rather absurd notion that the Jewish Messiah should disdain to eat like a Jew? But if you happen to be a Jewish reader of this foreword, please double back now and reread the quoted first paragraph of Boyarin's chapter 3, especially its ending:

"The ideas of Trinity and incarnation, or certainly the germs of those ideas, were already present among Jewish believers well before Jesus came on the scene to incarnate in himself, as it were, those theological notions and take up his messianic calling." The Trinity a Jewish idea? The *incarnation* a Jewish idea? Yes, indeed! And if such thoughts as these seem unthinkable, I can only urge: read on. They may seem more thinkable after you read Boyarin's deeply informed analysis of the Jewish background to Jesus' application to himself of the strange title *Son of Man*, a designation that ought to mean simply "human being" but clearly, and paradoxically, bespeaks divinity far more than does the more modest, merely royal or messianic designation *Son of God*.

The challenge that Daniel Boyarin delivers to Christians is, first, to surrender some of their claim to religious originality and, second, to think with him past a supposed Christian belief in the obliteration of nationality within the noble universality of the church. In an earlier book, *A Radical Jew: Paul and the Politics of Identity*, Boyarin urged Christians to remember that the same Paul who wrote

> There is no longer Jew or Greek, there is no longer slave or free, there is no longer male and female; for all of you are one in Christ Jesus. And if you belong

> to Christ, then you are Abraham's offspring, heirs according to the promise. (Galatians 3:28–29; New Revised Standard Version)

also wrote

> I ask, then, has God rejected his people? By no means! I myself am an Israelite, a descendant of Abraham, a member of the tribe of Benjamin. God has not rejected his people whom he foreknew (Romans 11:1–2; New Revised Standard Version).

Daniel Boyarin belongs to a generation of Jewish-American scholars who have addressed the Christian scriptures with an unprecedented and pathbreaking frankness and freedom. They see Paul, who boasted that as a pupil of Gamaliel [a famous early rabbi] he was "thoroughly trained in every point of our ancestral law" (Acts 22:3), as far more rabbinically Jewish than Jesus, contrary to an earlier view that saw him as sanitizing Jesus for Gentile consumption.

For Christians, true, the distinction between male and female is ultimately ephemeral because men and women are ultimately "one in Christ Jesus," but penultimately—which is to say, until the end of time—men and women do usually remain male and female, and Paul usually treated them as such. He was not the enemy of all difference. So also, then, for the difference between Jew and Gentile.

Titus, born Greek, could become a Christian Greek without undergoing circumcision, Paul stoutly insisted. Timothy, born Jewish but uncircumcised, had to be circumcised, Paul insisted by essentially the same token, so as to make a point for the benefit of Jews and Greeks alike. Timothy was to be a Christian, yes, but even as such he was to remain a Jew, a Christian Jew. In other words, the Jewish party was far from over when the Christian party began. On the contrary—and here is surely Boyarin's most mind-stretching correction—the Jews were the hosts, not the guests, at that Christian party, and what they were in practice at the start, he suggests, they can become again, at least in thought and in theory, even now.

Boyarin's challenge to Jews, then, is simply to recognize themselves or at least to imagine themselves in some semblance of this historic role, despite millennia of Christian scorn and persecution, despite even the Nazi Shoah, the ne plus ultra enactment of the malign and invidious thesis that Judaism and world Jewry are historically and existentially *over.* It is to recognize further that the Jewish engagement with Christianity has never, in fact, stopped at the null position of "what is new is not true, what is true is not new." More than that has always been happening between the womb-embattled twins, however ready Jewish leadership may have been to declare otherwise, for a powerful strand of Jewish thought has always wanted world engagement—a definitive and dramatic triumph upon the world religious stage. Thus did the Word of the Lord come to the prophet Zechariah saying:

> Thus said the LORD of Hosts: In those days, ten men from nations of every tongue will take hold—they will take hold of every Jew by a corner of his cloak and say, "Let us go with you, for we have heard that God is with you." (Zechariah 8:23; Jewish Publication Society *Tanakh*)

Ten *goyim* clinging to the elbow of every *yid*? How many Jews are ready for *that*? There is something undeniably comic about Zechariah's vision. It makes me think of Philip Roth's novel *Operation Shylock* in which a proponent of "Diasporism," a grandly eccentric dream of seeding Europe with new colonies of resettled Israelis, imagines how they will be received:

> "You know what will happen in Warsaw, at the railway station, when the first trainload of Jews returns? There will be crowds to welcome them. People will be jubilant. People will be in tears. They will be shouting, 'Our Jews are back! Our Jews are back!' The spectacle will be transmitted by television through the world." (*Operation Shylock*, p. 45)

But strange as it must seem, even comic as it must seem, some such motif is not alien to Israel's collective self-understanding. In the Book of Isaiah, the Lord God "who gathers the dispersed of Israel" does not stop there. He concludes, "I will gather still more to those already gathered" (Isaiah 56:8; Jewish Publication Society *Tanakh*), a line that comes at the end of a passage envisioning that the self-hating eunuchs and the cowed foreigners who imagine that they are unwelcome in the Temple of Solomon will someday know otherwise, for " 'My House shall be called a house of prayer for all peoples,' thus declares the LORD" (56:7).

Such a prospect is good for a laugh, good for the kind of laugh the family laughed in my parable at the snapshot of Ben—Ben the family football player—singing the national anthem as the music teacher's favorite boy soprano, good for the kind of laugh they laughed at the shot of Josh— Josh the family minstrel—in his football equipment. But the family album (*read*, here, their respective scriptures) didn't lie, did it? Ben's treble did soar that day at "land of the *freeee*," and Josh—didn't he actually score a touchdown in that game? Their history—their shared early life, as retained in the family album—concealed important clues to further possibilities in their adult lives. It just took the patience and the diligence of a Mr. Boyarin to see it.

Patient and diligent Daniel Boyarin has been through, by now, decades of scholarly endeavor. And it takes patience and diligence for even an intellectually prepared reader to assimilate what he has done, as any serious reader of his massive *Border Lines: The Partition of Judaeo-Christianity* will testify. The book before you, however, *The Jewish Gospels*, is by design inviting rather than daunting. It is the user-friendliest book that Daniel has ever written, and perhaps the user-friendliest that he will ever write. Think of it as a bracingly short sail on rough seas under a captain of uncompromising competence, unsparing candor, unconventional procedures, but, beneath it all, unfailing goodwill and good humor. Back on shore, count on it, you will be breathless and sunburned, but you'll have seen land and sea—Christianity and Judaism—as you never saw them before.

Bon voyage.

Acknowledgments

I wish to thank the following friends who have helped me enormously in the production of this book over the years in which it gestated: Carlin Barton, Adela Yarbro Collins, John J. Collins, Susan Griffin, Joel Marcus, John R. Miles, Andy Ross (much more than an agent), Ishay Rosen-Zvi, Eliyahu Stern, and especially Marc Favreau (much more than an editor). This book has had a very nurturing gestational period. Among the prime nurturing environments are counted four meetings of the Enoch Seminar and its maestro, Gabriele Boccacinni, and two summer seminars at the Wissenschaft Kolleg in Greifswald, wonderfully organized and conducted by Andreas Bedenbender, who deserves better of academia. I thank, as well, all of the participants in those several meetings severally and collectively. None are guaranteed to endorse the final results, and some are sure to disagree with them more or less sharply.

—*Greenfield*
July 2011

Introduction

IF THERE IS ONE THING that Christians know about their religion, it is that it is not Judaism. If there is one thing that Jews know about their religion, it is that it is not Christianity. If there is one thing that both groups know about this double not, it is that Christians believe in the Trinity and the incarnation of Christ (the Greek word for Messiah) and that Jews don't, that Jews keep kosher and Christians don't.

If only things were this simple. In this book, I'm going to tell a very different historical story, a story of a time when Jews and Christians were much more mixed up with each other than they are now, when there were many Jews who believed in something quite like the Father and the Son and even in something quite like the incarnation of the Son in the Messiah, and when followers of Jesus kept kosher as Jews, and accordingly a time in which the question of the difference between Judaism and Christianity just didn't exist as it does now. Jesus, when he came, came in a form that many, many Jews were expecting: a

1

second divine figure incarnated in a human. The question was not "Is a divine Messiah coming?" but only "Is this carpenter from Nazareth the One we are expecting?" Not surprisingly, some Jews said yes and some said no. Today we call the first group Christians and the second group Jews, but it was not like that then, not at all.

Everybody then—both those who accepted Jesus and those who didn't—was Jewish (or Israelite, the actual ancient terminology). Actually, there was no Judaism at all, nor was there Christianity. In fact, the idea of "a religion," that is, one of a number of religions to which one might or might not belong, had not come on the scene yet and wouldn't for centuries. By the third century (or even earlier) Christianity became a name for what Christians called themselves, but Jews were not to have a name for their religion in one of their own languages until sometime in the modern period, perhaps the eighteenth or nineteenth century. Until then terms meaning Judaism as the religion of the Jews were used only by non-Jews.

So, then, what are we talking about? We are not talking about a separate institution, a separate sphere of "religion," still less of a "faith" for Jews. We are talking about the complex of rituals and other practices, beliefs and values, history and political loyalties that constituted allegiance to the People of Israel, not a religion called Judaism. To get a sense of the absurdity of the proposition that Judaism is a religion the way Christianity is, let me consider a very recent event. In March 2011, the *New York Times* published the results of a social scientific study of satisfaction with life among various groups in the United States. Asian Americans were considered to be the "happiest" ethnic group, while Jews were considered to be the "happiest" religious group, thus leading to the inexorable conclusion that Asian American Jews were the happiest folk in America. This result is obviously flawed, because we all sense that both Jews and Asian Americans are ethnicities, whereas Christianity is never considered as an ethnic category at all. In fact, for us Jewishness is a very mixed category that doesn't really map onto either ethnicity or religion alone. This has a good historical basis. As Paula Fredriksen has recently written, "In antiquity . . . cult is an ethnic designation; ethnicity is a cultic designation."[1] That remained the case for Jews right up into modernity and to a not inconsiderable extent remains so even now.[2] In this book, the term "Judaism" will be used as a convenience to refer to that part of Jewish life that was concerned with obedience to God, worship, and belief, though I recognize that the term is an anachronism.

The Temple in Jerusalem was one of the most impressive cultic centers of the ancient world and famous throughout the known world for its splendor and magnificence. As opposed to most other peoples, who had many cultic centers, the Israelites performed all of their sacrifices at one place, the Temple in Jerusalem, for centuries—from

Josiah's reform in the seventh century B.C. until the Second Temple was destroyed in A.D. 70—(at least officially). When the Temple was extant, most Jews organized their religious lives around its festivals and rites, its priests and practices; distant Jews in Alexandria and similar places sent in donations. At least in principle, all Israelites were expected to make a pilgrimage to the one Temple in Jerusalem three times a year to celebrate the great festivals. This provided an organizing and joining principle for all the people transcending many disagreements and diversities. Even this, however, was not always the case, as there were groups, such as the people of the Dead Sea Scrolls, who rejected the Jerusalem Temple as corrupt.

Once the Temple was destroyed in A.D. 70, however, all bets were off. Some Jews wished to continue sacrifices as best they could, while others rejected such practices entirely. Some Jews thought that the purity practices that were important in Temple times were still to be practiced, while others thought they were irrelevant. There were, moreover, different interpretations of the Torah, different sets of ideas about God, different notions of how to practice the Law. In Jerusalem, which had been refounded by priests and teachers (scribes) returned from the Babylonian Exile (538 B.C.), new religious ideas and practices had been developed, many of them adopted by a group called the Pharisees, who were apparently rather aggressively promoting these ideas among Jews outside of Jerusalem who had different traditional practices, the so-called People of the Land, those who had not gone into Exile in Babylonia.

So being religiously Jewish then was a much more complicated affair than it is even now. There were no Rabbis yet, and even the priests in Jerusalem and around the countryside were divided among themselves. Not only that, but there were many Jews both in Palestine and outside of it, in places such as Alexandria in Egypt, who had very different ideas about what being a good, devout Jew meant. Some believed that in order to be a kosher Jew you had to believe in a single divine figure and any other belief was simply idol worship. Others believed that God had a divine deputy or emissary or even son, exalted above all the angels, who functioned as an intermediary between God and the world in creation, revelation, and redemption. Many Jews believed that redemption was going to be effected by a human being, an actual hidden scion of the house of David—an Anastasia—who at a certain point would take up the scepter and the sword, defeat Israel's enemies, and return her to her former glory. Others believed that the redemption was going to be effected by that same second divine figure mentioned above and not a human being at all. And still others believed that these two were one and the same, that the Messiah of David would be the divine Redeemer. As I said, a complicated affair.

While by now almost everyone, Christian and non-Christian, is happy enough to refer to Jesus, the human, as a Jew, I want to go a step beyond that. I wish us to see that Christ too—the divine Messiah—is a Jew. Christology, or the early ideas about Christ, is also a Jewish discourse and not—until much later—an anti-Jewish discourse at all. Many Israelites at the time of Jesus were expecting a Messiah who would be divine and come to earth in the form of a human. Thus the basic underlying thoughts from which both the Trinity and the incarnation grew are there in the very world into which Jesus was born and in which he was first written about in the Gospels of Mark and John.

You may well wonder why these distinctions—drawn from a very distant past—should matter to anyone in the present day. One difference that I expect this discussion to make is that Jews and Christians will need to begin to tell different stories about each other in the future. On one hand, Christians will no longer be able to claim that Jews willfully, as a body, rejected Jesus as God. Such beliefs about Jews have led to a deep, painful, and bloody history of anti-Judaism and anti-Semitism. Many ancient Jews simply accepted Jesus as God, and they did so because their beliefs and expectations had led them there. Others, while holding similar ideas about God, found it hard to believe that this particular, seemingly undistinguished, Jew was the one they were waiting for.

On the other hand, Jews will have to stop vilifying Christian ideas about God as simply a collection of "un-Jewish," perhaps pagan, and in any case bizarre fantasies.

God in a human body indeed! Recognizing these ideas as deeply rooted in the ancient complex of Jewish religious ideas may not lead us Jews to accept them but should certainly help us realize that Christian ideas are not alien to us; they are our own offspring and sometimes, perhaps, among the most ancient of all Israelite-Jewish ideas. On the other hand, certain kinds of modern "liberal" Christian apologists, such as Philip Pullman (the author of *His Dark Materials*), will have to stop separating out a "good Jesus" from a "bad Christ." I suggest that Jesus and Christ were one from the very beginning of the Jesus movement. It won't be possible any longer to think of some ethical religious teacher who was later promoted to divinity under the influence of alien Greek notions, with his so-called original message being distorted and lost; the idea of Jesus as divine-human Messiah goes back to the very beginning of the Christian movement, to Jesus himself, and even before that.

Checklists and Families: Christian and Non-Christian Jews

The terms "Christian Jews" and "non-Christian Jews" that I distinguish throughout this book might be surprising to people who think of Christians and Jews as opposites. But if we look closely at the first few centuries after Christ, we begin to see that this is precisely the way we ought to view the history of the religion of the Jews at that time. Before we get there, however, it may be helpful to challenge some of our closely held assumptions about what religions are.

For moderns, religions are fixed sets of convictions with well-defined boundaries. We usually ask ourselves: What convictions does Christianity forbid or what practices does it require? We ask similar questions in regard to Judaism, Hinduism, Islam, and Buddhism, the so-called great religions of the world. Such an understanding, of course, makes nonsense of the idea that one could be both a Jew and a Christian, rendering it just a contradiction in terms. Jews don't fit the definition of Christians, and Christians don't fit the definition of Jews. There are simple incompatibilities between these two religions that make it impossible to be both. I will argue in this book that this conception just doesn't always fit the facts, and specifically that it doesn't represent well the situation of Judaism and Christianity in the early centuries at all.

We usually define members of religions by using a kind of checklist. For instance, one could say that if someone believes in the Trinity and incarnation, she is a member of the religion Christianity, but if she doesn't, she isn't a proper member of that religion. One could say, conversely, that if someone does not believe in the Trinity and incarnation, then he is a member of the religion Judaism, but if he does believe in those things, he isn't. One could also say that if someone keeps the Sabbath on Saturday, eats only kosher food, and circumcises her sons, she is a member of the Jewish religion, but if she doesn't, she is not a member of the Jewish religion. Or, conversely again, if some group believes that everyone should keep the Sabbath, eat only kosher food, and circumcise sons, they are not Christians, but if they believe that these practices have been superseded, then they are Christians. This is, as I have said, our usual way of looking at such matters.

However, this manner of categorizing people's religions runs into difficulties. First, someone has to be making the checklists. Who decides what specific beliefs disqualify a person from being a Jew? Throughout history these decisions have been made by certain groups of people or individuals and are then imposed on other people (who may, however, refuse—unless the deciders have an army). It's a little bit like those "race" checklists on the census forms. Some of us simply refuse to check a box that defines us as Caucasian or Hispanic or African American because we don't identify that way, and only laws, and courts, or an army could force us to if they chose to. Of course, it will be asserted that the decisions about Jews and Christians (not Americans) were made by God and revealed in this Scripture or that, by this prophet or that, but this is a matter of faith, not of scholarship. Neither faith nor theology should play a role in the attempt to describe what was, as opposed to what ought to have been (according to this religious authority or another).

Another big problem these checklists cannot address

has to do with people whose beliefs and behaviors are a blend of characteristics from the two lists. In the case of Jews and Christians, this has been a problem that simply won't go away. For centuries after Jesus' death, there were people who believed in Jesus' divinity as the incarnate Messiah but who also insisted that in order to be saved they must eat only kosher, keep the Sabbath as other Jews do, and circumcise their sons. Here was an environment where many people, it would seem, thought that there was no problem in being both a Jew and a Christian. Moreover, many of the very items that would form the eventual checklist for being a Jew or being a Christian did not at all form a border line at that time. What shall we do with these folks?

For quite a number of generations after the coming of Christ, different followers and groups of followers of Jesus held many different theological views and engaged in a great variety of practices with respect to the Jewish law of their ancestors. One of the most important arguments had to do with the relation between the two entities who would end up being the first two persons of the Trinity. Many Christians believed that the Son or the Word (Logos) was subordinate to God the Father and even created by him; others believed that while the Son was uncreated and had existed from before the beginning of time, he nonetheless was only of a *similar* substance to the Father; a third group believed that there was no difference at all in substance between the Father and the Son. There were also very sharp differences in practice between Christian and Christian: some Christians kept much of the Jewish law (or all of it), some kept some rules but dropped others (e.g., the apostolic rule of Acts), and still others believed that the entire law needed to be overturned and discarded by Christians (even those born Jews). Finally, there were Christians who held that Easter was a form of the Jewish Passover, suitably interpreted with Jesus as the Lamb of God and paschal sacrifice, while others vigorously denied such connections. These had an analogue in practice as well, with the former group celebrating Easter at the same time as the Jews celebrated Passover, while the latter just as vigorously insisted that Easter must *not* be when the Jews hold their Passover. There were many other points of conflict as well. Until early in the fourth century, all of these different groups and diverse individuals called themselves Christians, and quite a few called themselves both Jews and Christians as well.

Checklists and the Imperial Religion

The checklist approach to making an absolute divide between Christian and non-Christian, between Jew and non-Jew, came into its own under the Christian Roman Empire, which set much store in getting all the messiness sorted out.

For many years it was believed that an early period of fluidity came to an end in a definitive "parting of the ways" that took place in either the first or second century. The argument was twofold. On one hand, the Temple had been such a unifying force that other forms of diversity were much more tolerable without threatening the core of Jewish identity. Following the destruction of the Jerusalem Temple by the Romans in A.D. 70, other ways had to be produced to secure such identity, hence the invention of a Jewish orthodoxy that excluded followers of Jesus. On the other hand, we are told that it was the divergence of Christianity from that core that drove an early parting of the ways. I contend that such diversity did not end with the destruction of the Temple and continued well beyond this event. Many have thought until recently (and some still do) that it ended with the Council of Yavneh, which allegedly took place in A.D. 90 or so.[3] According to a certain interpretation of a talmudic legend, this was a great Jewish ecumenical council (something like the great Christian ecumenical councils of the fourth and fifth centuries) in which all sectarian differences were abolished: all Jews agreed to follow the pharisaic-rabbinic tradition, and those who didn't were expelled and left the Jewish polity. But this view has largely been discredited by recent scholarship. It was invented by scholars more or less on the model of the great late-ancient Christian councils during which Christian orthodoxy was promulgated, especially the famous Council of Nicaea and its successor the Council of Constantinople.

In 381 at Constantinople the definitive step in cleaning up the differences based on a half century of negotiations following the Council of Nicaea was taken.[4] In 318 the newly Christian emperor Constantine had called an ecumenical council of bishops from all over the Christian world to come to Nicaea (present-day İznik in Turkey) to sort all of this out and restore peace to the Christian churches and communities, following a great deal of dissension, conflict, and bitterness between them.

Some of the major issues addressed at Nicaea were matters of creed, such as the precise definition of the relationship between the Father and the Son. Others were matters of practice, such as the correct date of Easter and its relationship to the Jewish Passover. It was here, at Nicaea, that on the first question it was decided that the Son was consubstantial with the Father, that is, they are two persons of the exact same divine substance. Easter was severed once and for all within orthodox churches from its calendrical and thematic connections with Passover. In the end what was accomplished in Nicaea and Constantinople was the establishment of a Christianity that was completely separated from Judaism. Since Christianity could not define its borders on the basis of ethnicity, geographical location, or even birth, finding clear ways to separate itself from Judaism was very urgent—and these councils pursued this end vigorously. This had the secondary historical effect of putting the power of the Roman Empire and its church authorities behind the existence of a fully separate "orthodox" Judaism as well. At least from a juridical standpoint, then, Judaism and Christianity became completely separate religions in the fourth century. Before that, no one (except God, of course) had the authority to tell folks that they were or were not Jewish or Christian, and many had chosen to be both. At the time of Jesus, all who followed Jesus—and even those who believed that he was God—were Jews!

The decisions that were made in Nicaea had the effect, as well, of driving a powerful wedge between traditional Jewish beliefs and practices and the newly invented orthodox Christianity. By defining the Son as entirely on an equal footing with the Father and by insisting that Easter had no connection with Passover, both of these aims were realized. Between Nicaea and Constantinople, many folks who considered themselves Christians were written right out of Christianity. Christians who practiced Judaism, even only by holding Easter at Passover (which included practically the entire church of Asia Minor for a few centuries), especially were declared heretics. Nicaea effectively created what we now understand to be Christianity, and, oddly enough, what we now understand as Judaism as well.

Across the seven decades between the Councils of

Nicaea and Constantinople, options for ways of believing or being Christians were cut off through this process of selection, especially the option to be both Christian and Jew at the same time. One could not both believe in Jesus and go to synagogue on Sabbath: we won't let you. Also, say the Nicene rulers of the Church, one must believe that the Father and the Son are separate persons but of exactly the same substance. God from God, as the formula goes; if you don't, say these rulers, you are not a Christian but a Jew and a heretic. These strenuous efforts to make the separation absolute were further productive of a great deal of anti-Jewish discourse at the time and continuing almost to our own day (nor is it quite dead yet). Bishop John Chrysostom's (c. 349–407) sermons "Against the Jews" were an excellent example of this development.[5]

One of the most zealous defenders of the new orthodoxy was St. Jerome. Not exactly a household name, Jerome (A.D. 347–420) was nonetheless one of the most important Christian scholars, thinkers, and writers of the late fourth and early fifth centuries. Considered one of the four "doctors of the Church" by the Roman Church,* he translated the Bible from Hebrew and Greek into the

---

* Notes the *Catholic Encyclopedia*: "Certain ecclesiastical writers have received this title on account of the great advantage the whole Church has derived from their doctrine. In the Western church four eminent Fathers of the Church attained this honour in the early Middle Ages: St. Gregory the Great, St. Ambrose, St. Augustine, and St. Jerome."

Latin Vulgate (this translation continues to be the official Latin Bible of the Catholic Church). He also was one of the most important translators of important early Greek Christian writers into Latin (especially the works of Origen).

We have a wonderful, lively collection of his letters written to his more famous colleague St. Augustine of Hippo, a fellow doctor of the Roman Church, on the best strategies for defending this new orthodoxy. In one of these letters, he stated:

> In our own day there exists a sect among the Jews throughout all the synagogues of the East, which is called the sect of the Minei, and is even now condemned by the Pharisees. The adherents to this sect are known commonly as Nazarenes; they believe in Christ the Son of God, born of the Virgin Mary; and they say that He who suffered under Pontius Pilate and rose again, is the same as the one in whom we believe. But while they desire to be both Jews and Christians, they are neither the one nor the other.[6]

A close look at Jerome's text will explain several of the points that I have been making. Jerome described a group of people who believed in the orthodox Nicene Creed: Christ is the son of God, he was born of a virgin, he was crucified and suffered, he rose. But they thought they were Jews too—they prayed in synagogues, kept the

Sabbath, and adhered to dietary and other rules. In fact, they didn't see "Christians" and "Jews" as two categories at all but as one complex category. Presumably they were practicing some sort of Jewish ritual as well, although it is unclear from Jerome's statement precisely what it was. Jerome denied them their claim of being Christian, because they claimed to be Jews; he denied them their claim to be Jews, because they claimed to be Christians. And he certainly denied them the possibility of being both, because that was an impossibility in Jerome's worldview. For him (and for us as well), these were mutually exclusive possibilities. However, for these Jews who confessed the Nicene Creed, there was no contradiction. Just as today there are Jews who are Hassidic—some of whom believe that the Messiah has come, died, and will be resurrected—and Jews who reject the Hassidic movement entirely but all are considered Jews, so in antiquity there were Jews who were believers in Christ and Jews who weren't, but all were Jews. To use another comparison that is evocative if not entirely exact, it is as if non-Christian Jews and Christian Jews were more like Catholics and Protestants today than like Jews and Christians today—parts of one religious grouping, not always living in harmony or recognizing each other's legitimacy but still in a very important sense apprehensible as one entity.

In order to protect the orthodox notion that there is an absolute distinction between Jews and Christians,

Jerome had to "invent" a third category, neither Christians nor Jews. Jerome, backed up by the fiats of Emperor Constantine's Council of Nicaea and the law of the Roman Empire, the code of the Emperor Theodosius, rather imperiously declared that some folks were simply not Christians; even more surprisingly, he claimed he could decide that they were not Jews either, because they didn't fit his definition of Jews. No one before Constantine had had the power to declare some folks not Christians or not Jews.

Jerome tells us something about the synagogue leadership here as well: they also condemned these people as not Jews, thus applying a similar type of checklist to read people out of a group.

But there's more yet. Jerome gives fascinating names to this sect of not-Jews, not-Christians. He calls them, as we've seen, *minei* and Nazarenes. These names, mysterious as they seem at first, are really not mysteries at all. They refer to two terms used in the rabbinic prayer against the sectarians, which is, in fact, first firmly attested in Jerome's fifth century (although earlier forms of it are known from the third century). In this prayer, repeated in the synagogues, Jews used to say: "And to the *minim* and to the *Notzrim*, let there be no hope."

The term *minim* means, literally, "kinds." Jews who don't belong to the group that the Rabbis wish to define as kosher are named by them as "kinds" of Jews, not entirely mainstream. This included Jews who are not quite halakhically/theologically correct, such as followers of Jesus, but still Jews. The second term, *Notzrim* (Latinized as *Nazarenes*), is much more specific, referring as it does to Nazareth and thus explicitly to Christians. This is plausibly the very prayer to which Jerome is referring in his letter, since his alleged condemnation by the Pharisees comprises precisely these two names for the group. The word *minim* seems just to mean sectarians in a general sense, including such as these who follow the Jewish law but confess the Nicene Creed. The word *Notzrim* (Nazarenes) would be a specific reference to that Christian character of these Jews. But according to Jerome's report, even this is not a Jewish condemnation of Christians in general but rather applies to those poor folks who couldn't tell the difference properly and thought that they were both.[7] The total delegitimation that Jerome seeks to accomplish of the both-Jews-and-Christians in his letter to Augustine by declaring them "nothing," the Rabbis (whom he calls anachronistically "Pharisees") seek to accomplish through the medium of a curse against those same Jews-and-Christians when they come to the synagogue. While both would undoubtedly have denied it angrily, Jerome and the Rabbis are engaged in a kind of conspiracy to delegitimate these folks who defined themselves as both Jewish and Christians, in order that the checklists remain absolutely clear and unambiguous.

As we can see, these seemingly innocuous checklists are really tools of power, not simply description. If, thunders Jerome, you believe in the Nicene Creed, get out of the synagogue, and you will be a Christian. If you stay in the synagogue and drop your belief in Christian doctrine, then the Pharisees will agree to call you a Jew. Fill in the boxes correctly on the checklist, or you are neither a Christian nor a Jew. The very fact that Jerome and the Rabbis needed to fight against these *minim*, these Nazarenes who thought they were both Jews and Christians, suggests that they did, in fact, exist and in sufficient numbers to arouse concern.

We need a way of thinking about the varieties of Jewish religious experience—especially in the crucial early period—that successfully accounts for the eddying and swirling of different currents of thought in a larger, more complex field of differences and similarities, one that enables us to speak of both the Rabbis and the *Notzrim* as historically—not normatively—expressions of Judaism.

Instead of a checklist for who is a Jew, which inevitably, as we have seen, leads to arbitrary exclusions, we could use the idea of family resemblances in order to recapture the period of religious fluidity that followed Jesus' death. As one literary scholar has noted, "Members of one family share a variety of similar features: eyes, gait, hair color, temperament. But—and this is the crucial point—there need be no one set of features shared by all family members."[8] There is perhaps one feature that constitutes all as members of the Judeo-Christian family, namely, appealing to the Hebrew Scriptures as revelation. Similarly, there was one feature that could be said to be common to all ancient groups that we might want to call (anachronistically) Christian, namely, some form of discipleship to Jesus. Yet this feature hardly captures enough richness and depth to produce a descriptively productive category, for in so many other vitally important ways, groups that followed Jesus and groups that ignored him were similar to each other. To put this point another way, groups that ignored or rejected Jesus may have had some highly salient other features (for instance, belief in the Son of Man) that bound them to Jesus groups and disconnected them from other non-Jesus Jews. On the other hand, some Jesus Jews may have had aspects to their religious lives (following pharisaic, or even rabbinic, halakha) that drew them closer to some non-Jesus Jews than to other Jesus People.[9] Moreover, some Jesus groups might have related to Jesus in ways more similar to the ways that other non-Jesus Jewish groups related to other prophets, leaders, or Messiahs than to the ways that other Jesus groups were relating to Jesus. That is, some Jews in the first century in Palestine might have been expecting a Messiah who would be an incarnation of the divine but rejected Jesus as the one, while some other Jews who accepted Jesus might have thought of him not as divine but only as a human Messiah. The model of family resemblance therefore seems apt for talking about a Judaism that incorporates early Christianity as well. This expanded understanding of "Judaism" completely allows for the inclusion of the earliest Gospel literature within its purview, thus making the earliest and in some ways most foundational texts of Christianity—Jewish.

The Jewish Gospels

By now, almost everyone recognizes that the historical Jesus was a Jew who followed ancient Jewish ways.[10] There is also growing recognition that the Gospels themselves and even the letters of Paul are part and parcel of the religion of the People of Israel in the first century A.D. What is less recognized is to what extent the ideas surrounding what we call Christology, the story of Jesus as the divine-human Messiah, were also part (if not parcel) of Jewish diversity at this time.

The Gospels themselves, when read in the context of other Jewish texts of their times, reveal this very complex diversity and attachment to other variants of "Judaism" at the time. There are traits that bind the Gospel of Matthew to one strain of first-century "Judaism" while other traits bind the Gospel of John to other strains. The same goes for Mark, and even for Luke, which is generally considered the "least Jewish" of the Gospels.

By blurring the boundaries between "Jews" and "Christians," we are making clearer the historical situation and development of early "Judaism" and Christianity. We can understand much better the significance of our historical documents, including the Gospels, when we imagine a state of affairs that more properly reflects the social situation on the ground of that time, a social situation in which believers in Jesus of Nazareth and those who didn't follow him were mixed up with each other in various ways rather than separated into two well-defined entities that we know today as Judaism and Christianity.

Among those different types of Jews, we will find "proselytes, God-fearers, and *gerim*."[11] The "proselytes" were non-Jews who completely threw their lot in with the Jewish people and became Jews, while the "God-fearers" remained identified as Greeks and pagans but adhered to the God of Israel and the synagogue because they admired the religion of the One God. The *gerim*, sojourners or resident aliens, were Gentiles who lived among Jews in "their" land. As such, they were required to observe certain laws of the Torah and received certain protections and privileges as well. It has been recently pointed out that the *gerim* were required to keep precisely the laws marked out in Acts for Gentile followers of Jesus, thus giving even these a place in the household of Israel. Talking about the borders of Judaism and Christianity is much more complicated (and interesting) than we might have thought previously.

Belief in Jesus was one of many overlapping forms of the complex of practices and convictions that we today call Judaism. But it is no longer clear that even this is the most interesting or important difference among various Jewish groups as seen from that time, as opposed to a view from our time with all the history that has intervened. Jews who didn't accept Jesus of Nazareth shared many ideas with Jews who did, including ideas that today mark off any absolute difference between two religions, Judaism and Christianity. Some of these ideas were very close, if not identical, to the ideas of the Father and the Son and even the incarnation. Not to pay attention to this is to continue to commit the theologically founded anachronism of seeing Jews (and thus Jewish Jesus folk also) as more or less "Jewish" insofar as they approach the religion—verbal and embodied practices—of the Rabbis.

My story is one of possibilities cut off by authorities, both orthodox Christian leaders such as Jerome on the one hand and "orthodox"—for Judaism the term is an anachronism and maybe even a misnomer—rabbinic or "Pharisaic" authorities on the other. What revisiting those possibilities might augur cannot be predicted in advance. One of those most secure ideas about the absolute difference between Judaism and Christianity is that Christians believe that Jesus was the Son of God. So let's begin our journey there.

1

From Son of God to Son of Man

WHO WAS JESUS? The conventional view, of course, is that "Son of God" is the decisive title for Jesus. It is by this title that Jesus is held to be part of the Trinity: Father, Son, and Holy Spirit. It is as the Son of God that he is worshipped as divine; it is as the Son of God that he was deemed to have been given to be sacrificed in order that the world might be redeemed. But things are not quite that simple. First of all, interestingly enough, the term "Son of God" is not often used to refer to Jesus in the New Testament. In Paul, the much more common term is "Lord." In the Gospels, Jesus is more likely to be referred to (or actually to refer to himself) by the title "Son of Man." Most Christians today, if they have thought about it at all, would think that by this title, Son of Man, Jesus' human nature is being designated, while the title "Son of God" refers to his divine nature. This was indeed the interpretation of most of the Fathers of the Church. A new Bible translation called the Common English Bible has gone so far as to translate "Son of Man" as "the human one." In this chapter, I will show that *almost* the opposite was the case in the Gospel of Mark: "Son of God" referred to the king of Israel, the earthly king of David's seat, while "Son of Man" referred to a heavenly figure and not a human being at all.

. The title "Son of Man" denoted Jesus as a part of God, while the title "Son of God" indicated his status as King Messiah. But what is the Messiah and how does it relate to the Christ? Truth be told, they were exactly the same thing, or at any rate the same word. *Messiah* (in Hebrew pronounced "mashiach") means "anointed one," no more or less, and *Christos* is simply a Greek translation of that very word, meaning also "anointed one." As the Gospel of John tells us forthrightly: "He first findeth his own brother Simon, and saith unto him, We have found the Messias," which is, being translated, the Christ (John 1:41).*

The Messiah Son of God as Human King

The reason that the king was called the Messiah was because he was literally anointed with oil at the time of his

---

* This is the way most translators have translated the term, as a Jewish-Greek equivalent of *Messiah*, and it seems to me correct. Some more recent translators translate it literally as "anointed," which is not the value that the term had in Hebrew by the first century, let alone in Greek.

accession to the kingdom. One of the best examples of this enthronement ceremony is to be found in the Book of Samuel:

> Then Samuel took the vial of oil, and poured it upon his head, and kissed him, and said, Is it not that YHVH has anointed you to be prince over his inheritance? (1 Samuel 10:1)

Samuel pours a vial of oil over the head of Saul and then explicitly names him King of Israel. This king of Israel has been appointed by God to be the ruler of Israel, to be charismatic, and to represent Israel before God. Through the medium of the prophet Samuel, God himself has anointed Saul with oil to be the king over his inheritance, Israel. The king is therefore referred to in the Hebrew Bible as the Anointed of YHVH or the Mashiach of YHVH. Other Israelite kings who are described as having been anointed with oil on their accession to the kingship include David (1 Samuel 16:3), Solomon (1 Kings 1:34), Jehu (1 Kings 19:16), Joash (2 Kings 11:12), and Jehoahaz (2 Kings 23:30). As pointed out by the dean of Catholic biblical scholars in the United States, Joseph Fitzmyer, SJ, nowhere in the Hebrew Bible does this usage imply anything but the extraordinarily close connection between the King of Israel and the God of Israel. No awaited or future divine king is contemplated in any of these instances.[1]

The term Mashiach throughout the Hebrew Bible means a historical actually reigning human king of Israel, neither more nor less. The "prince" of 1 Samuel's Saul evolved (not without struggle) into the full-blown monarch of the dynasty of David during the period of the Kings, and the term "Anointed of YHVH" (Messiah, Christos) is one of his titles.

The point that the Messiah in the Hebrew Bible always refers to an actually ruling historical king is particularly significant when we consider the following verses:

> Kings of the earth set themselves up, and rulers conspire together against YHVH and against his anointed one (his Mashiach). . . . "I have installed my king on Zion, my holy hill." I will recount the decree of YHVH: He said to me, "You are my son; this day I have begotten you." (Psalms 2:2, 6–7)

The anointed, earthly king of Israel is adopted by God as his son; the son of God is thus the reigning, living king of Israel. "This day I have begotten you" means this day you have been enthroned.[2] Militating against any literal sense in which the king was taken as son of God and divine is the "this day," which, it seems, may only mean on this the day of your accession to the throne. Another moment in the Psalms where we find the King as the Son of God is in the crucial verses of Psalm 110 (the very verses that also contribute the notion of the exalted Christ seated at the right hand of Power [Mark 14:62]). In this Psalm we read, "In sacred splendor, from the womb, from dawn, you have the dew wherewith I have begotten you." This verse is notoriously difficult, and I shan't here go into the complications of its emendations and interpretations, but one thing seems clear: God says to the king here too, "I have begotten you."[3] The bottom line of this demonstration is that early on the term "Son of God" was used to refer to the Davidic king without any hints of incarnation of the deity in the king: "I will be to you as a father, and you will be to me as a son." The king is indeed very intimate with God and a highly sacralized person—but not God. The kingship is promised to David's seed forever.

Something rather dramatic and tragic happened, however, in the history of the People of Israel. During the sixth century B.C., the kingdom of the Lord's anointed ones in Jerusalem was destroyed and the Davidic line was lost. As the story is narrated in 2 Kings 25, following a siege in 597 B.C., Nebuchadnezzar had installed Zedekiah as tributary king of Judah. However, Zedekiah revolted against Babylon. Nebuchadnezzar responded by invading Judah and began a siege of Jerusalem in January 589 B.C. In 587 B.C., the eleventh year of Zedekiah's reign, Nebuchadnezzar broke through Jerusalem's walls, conquering the city. Zedekiah and his followers attempted to escape but were captured on the plains of Jericho and taken to Riblah. There, after seeing his sons killed, Zedekiah was blinded, bound, and taken captive to Babylon, where he remained a prisoner until his death. After the fall of Jerusalem, the Babylonian general Nebuzaraddan was sent to complete its destruction. Jerusalem was plundered and Solomon's Temple was destroyed. Most of the elite were taken into captivity in Babylon. The city was razed to the ground. Some Israelite people were permitted to remain to tend to the land.

The people—and especially its leadership—went into exile in Babylonia, and even when they were allowed to come back, less than a century later, there was no more Davidic kingdom and no glorious king ruling in Jerusalem. The people prayed for such a king to rule over them once again and for a restoration of that earthly glory. It is, however, still an earthly and actual king for whom the people pray throughout the Hebrew Bible, for a restoration of the House of David as it was before the Exile. In this prayer for an absent king, for a new king of the House of David, the seeds, however, are planted of the notion of a promised Redeemer, a new King David whom God would send at the end of days. That notion would come to fruition in the time of the Second Temple.

When Mark in the very beginning of his Gospel writes, "The Beginning of the Gospel of Jesus Christ, the Son of God," the Son of God means the human Messiah, using the old title for the king of the House of David. When, on the other hand, Mark refers to him in the second chapter of the Gospel as the "Son of Man," he is pointing to the divine nature of the Christ. This seems like a paradox: the name of God being used for Jesus' human nature, the name of "Man" for his divine nature. How did it come about? This chapter begins to answer the question of how Jesus was understood as God by monotheistic Jews by telling the story of the Son of Man.

The Son of Man as Divine Redeemer

While the expectation of the restoration of the Davidic king was growing, other ideas about redemption were developing in Israel as well. In the seventh chapter of the Book of Daniel, written circa 161 B.C., we find a remarkable apocalyptic story. *Apocalypse* is a Greek-derived word that means "revelation" (the New Testament book that we call Revelation is also known as the Apocalypse). Generally in an apocalypse, the things that are revealed have to do with the end of days, with what will happen at the end of time and end of the world. The Book of Daniel is one of the earliest apocalypses that was ever written. Taking its clues from the prophet Ezekiel, it describes the heavenly visions of the prophet Daniel. The book was written sometime during the second century B.C. and became one of the most influential books for latter-day Jewry, including, perhaps even especially, in its Christian branch.

In this remarkable text, we find the prophet Daniel

having a vision in which there are two divine figures, one who is depicted as an old man, an Ancient of Days, sitting on the throne. We have been told, however, that there is more than one throne there, and sure enough a second divine figure, in form "like a human being," is brought on the clouds of heaven and invested by the Ancient of Days in a ceremony very much like the passing of the torch from elder king to younger in ancient Near Eastern royal ceremonial and the passing of the torch from older gods to younger ones in their myths: "I saw in the vision of the night, and behold with the clouds of the Heaven there came one like a Son of Man and came to the Ancient of Days and stood before him and brought him close, and to him was given rulership and the glory and the kingdom, and all nations, peoples, and languages will worship him. His rulership is eternal which will not pass, and his kingship will not be destroyed."

We can begin to see here a notion about redemption that is quite different from the expectation of the restoration of a Davidic king on the throne of Jerusalem. What this text projects is a second divine figure to whom will be given eternal dominion of the entire world, of a restored entire world in which this eternal king's guidance and rule will be in accord, completely and finally, with the will of the Ancient of Days as well. Although this Redeemer figure is not called the Messiah—this name for him will have to wait for later reflections on this Danielic vision, as we shall see below—it brings us close to at least some of the crucial characteristics of the figure named later the Messiah or the Christ.

What are these characteristics?

He is divine.
He is in human form.
He may very well be portrayed as a younger-
    appearing divinity than the Ancient of Days.
He will be enthroned on high.
He is given power and dominion, even sovereignty
    on earth.

All of these are characteristic of Jesus the Christ as he will appear in the Gospels, and they appear in this text more than a century and a half before the birth of Jesus. Moreover, they have been further developed within Jewish traditions between the Book of Daniel and the Gospels. At a certain point these traditions became merged in Jewish minds with the expectation of a return of a Davidic king, and the idea of a divine-human Messiah was born. This figure was then named "Son of Man," alluding to his origins in the divine figure named "one like a Son of Man/ a human being" in Daniel. In other words, a simile, a God who looks like a human being (literally Son of Man) has become the name for that God, who is now called "Son of Man," a reference to his human-appearing divinity. The only plausible explanation of the "Son of Man" is that of

Leo Baeck, the great Jewish theologian and scholar of the last century, who wrote: "Whenever in later works 'that Son of Man,' 'this Son of Man, or 'the Son of Man' is mentioned, it is the quotation from Daniel that is speaking."[4]

This dual background explains much of the complexity of the traditions about Jesus. It is no wonder, then, that when a man came who claimed and appeared in various ways to fit these characteristics, many Jews believed he was precisely the one whom they expected. (It's also no wonder that many were more skeptical.)

There are many variations of traditions about this figure in the Gospels themselves and in other early Jewish texts. Some Jews had been expecting this Redeemer to be a human exalted to the state of divinity, while others were expecting a divinity to come down to earth and take on human form; some believers in Jesus believed the Christ had been born as an ordinary human and then exalted to divine status, while others believed him to have been a divinity who came down to earth. Either way, we end up with a doubled godhead and a human-divine combination as the expected Redeemer.* The connections between older pre-Jesus ideas of the Messiah/Christ and those that Jesus would claim for himself are thus very intimate indeed.

---

* In these ideas lie the seed that would eventually grow into doctrines of the Trinity and incarnation in all of their later variations, variations that are inflected as well by Greek philosophical thinking; the seeds, however, were sown by Jewish apocalyptic writings.

Who Is the Son of Man?

Jesus famously refers to himself by that mysterious term "The Son of Man." Oceans of ink and forests of trees have given their substance so that humans could continue to argue about where this term came from and what it means.[5] Regarding its meaning, some say it refers to Jesus' human nature, while others say it refers to his divine nature. In the Middle Ages it was taken as a sign of Jesus' humility but later on was understood as such a potent mark of potentially blasphemous arrogance that many scholars have argued that the "Son of Man" sayings were all put into Jesus' mouth after his death. Some have argued that the term referred to a primordial heavenly man figure and was connected with Iranian religion, while others have denied entirely that there ever was such a figure at all. All this has added up to what has been called for generations now "The Son of Man Problem."

When Jesus came and walked around Galilee proclaiming himself the Son of Man, no one ever asked: "What is a Son of Man, anyway?" They knew what he was talking about whether they believed his claim or not, much as modern folks in many parts of the world would understand someone saying "I am the Messiah." But there is a puzzlement here, because the term is very odd in any of the ancient languages with which we are concerned—Hebrew, Aramaic, and Greek.

The Christological use of the term "the Son of Man" as a name for a specific figure is unintelligible in Hebrew and Aramaic as an ordinary linguistic usage. In those Semitic languages it is an ordinary word that means "human being"; in Greek it indicates, at best, somebody's child. One would think, then, that when Jesus referred to himself as the Son of Man, Aramaic-speakers would hear him just calling himself a person. But the contexts in Mark will not allow us to interpret Jesus' use of the term as meaning just a human being. It would be very difficult to interpret the verses of Mark 2 (discussed later in this chapter) as meaning that any old human has the capacity to forgive sins against God or that any person is Lord of the Sabbath.

Referring to an individual as the Son of Man therefore has to be explained historically and literarily. It only makes sense if "The Son of Man" was a known and recognized title in the world of the writer and characters in Mark. Whence came this title? All such usages must have been an allusion to the pivotal chapter in the book of Daniel.

Much New Testament scholarship has been led astray by an assumption that the term "Son of Man" referred only to the coming of Jesus on the clouds at the *parousia*, Jesus' expected reappearance on earth. This has led to much confusion in the literature, because on this view it seems difficult to imagine how the living, breathing Jesus, not yet the exalted-into-heaven or returning-to-earth Christ, could refer to *himself* as the Son of Man, as he surely seems to do in several places in Mark and the other Gospels. This problem can be solved, however, if we think of the Son of Man not as representing a particular stage in the narrative of the Christ but as referring to the protagonist of the entire story, Jesus the Christ, Messiah, Son of Man.

It has been frequently thought that the Son of Man designation refers only to the Messiah (the Christ) at the time of his exaltation and after. In Mark 14:61–62, the high priest asks of Jesus: "Are you the Messiah [Christ], the Son of the Blessed?" And Jesus said, "I am, and you will see the Son of Man seated at the right hand of Power, and coming with the clouds of heaven." One could easily understand from this verse that Jesus uses the title Son of Man to refer only to the moment in which you will see him coming with the clouds of heaven. Now if the Son of Man is, the reasoning goes, the Messiah (the Christ) seated at the right hand of Power and coming with the clouds of heaven, how could the term "Son of Man" have been used by Jesus to refer to his earthly life? The scholarship then has to go to great lengths to determine which of the Son of Man sayings Jesus could have, might have, or did say and which were added by the Early Church—the disciples or the evangelists—and put in his mouth. If, however, we understand that the designation Son of Man refers not to a single stage in the narrative of Jesus—birth, incarnation, sovereignty on earth, death, resurrection, or exaltation—but to all of these together, then these problems are entirely obviated. If Jesus (whether the "historical" Jesus or the Jesus portrayed in the Gospels) believed that he was the Son of Man, he was so from beginning to end of the story, not just at one moment within it. The Son of Man is the name of a narrative and its protagonist.

This narrative, the narrative that Jesus understood himself to embody, grows out of a reading of the story of the career of the "one like a Son of Man" in the Book of Daniel. In Daniel 7, we find the following account of the prophet's night vision:

> [9]As I watched, thrones were set in place, and an Ancient One took his throne, his clothing was white as snow, and the hair of his head like pure wool; his throne was fiery flames, and its wheels were burning fire. [10]A stream of fire issued and flowed out from his presence. A thousand thousands served him, and ten thousand times ten thousand stood attending him. The court sat in judgment, and the books were opened. . . . [13]As I watched in the night visions, I saw one like a son of man [human being] with the clouds of heaven. And he came to the Ancient One and was presented before him. [14]To him was given dominion and glory and kingship, that all peoples, nations, and languages should serve him. His dominion is an everlasting dominion that shall not pass away, and his kingship is one that shall never be destroyed.

In this prophetic narrative, we see two divine figures, one who is clearly marked as an ancient and one who has the appearance of a young human being. The younger one has his own throne (that's why there is more than one throne set up to start with), and he is invested by the older one with dominion, glory, and kingship over all the peoples of the world; not only that, but it will be an eternal kingship forever and ever. This is the vision that will become in the fullness of time the story of the Father and the Son.

From the earliest layers of interpretation and right up to modern times, some interpreters have deemed the "one like a son of man" a symbol of a collective, namely, the faithful Israelites at the time of the Maccabean revolt, when the Book of Daniel was probably written.[6] Other interpreters have insisted that the "[one like a] son of man" is a second divine figure alongside the Ancient of Days and not an allegorical symbol of the People of Israel. We find in Aphrahat, the fourth-century Iranian Father of the Church, the following attack on the interpretation (presumably by Jews) that makes the "one like a son of man" out to be the People of Israel: "Have the children of Israel received the kingdom of the Most High? God forbid! Or has that people come on the clouds of heaven?" (Demonstration 5:21) Aphrahat's argument is exegetical and very much to the point. Clouds—as well as riding on or with clouds—are a common attribute of biblical divine appearances, called theophanies (Greek for "God appearances") by scholars.[7] J.A. Emerton had made the point decisively: "The act of coming with clouds suggests a theophany of Yahwe himself. If Dan. vii.13 does not refer to a divine being, then it is the only exception out of about seventy passages in the O[ld] T[estament]."[8] It is almost impossible to read the narrative here of the setting up of thrones, the appearance of the Ancient of Days on one of them, and the coming to him of the one like a son of man apart from stories of the investiture of young gods by their elders, of close gods by transcendent ones.* Some modern scholars support Aphrahat unequivocally. As New Testament scholar Matthew Black puts it bluntly, "This, in effect, means that Dan. 7 knows of two divinities, the Head of Days and the Son of Man."[9] Those two divinities, in the course of time, would end up being the first two persons of the Trinity.

---

* Note that at least some of the later Rabbis also read this passage as a theophany (self-revelation of God). The following passage from the Babylonian Talmud (fifth or sixth century) clearly shows this and cites earlier Rabbis as well as seeing an important moment in the doctrine of God emerging here.

> One verse reads: "His throne is sparks of fire" (Dan. 7:9) and another [part of the] verse reads, "until thrones were set up and the Ancient of Days sat" (7:9). This is no difficulty: One was for him and one was for David.
>
> As we learn in an ancient tradition: One for him and one for David; these are the words of Rabbi Aqiva. Rabbi Yose the Galilean said to him: Aqiva! Until when will you make the Shekhina profane?! Rather. One was for judging and one was for mercy.

This clear and obviously correct interpretation would seem to be belied by the continuation of the Daniel 7 text itself, however:

> [15]As for me, Daniel, my spirit was troubled within me, and the visions of my head terrified me. [16]I approached one of the attendants to ask him the truth concerning all this. So he said that he would disclose to me the interpretation [*pesher*] of the matter: [17]"As for these four great beasts, four kings shall arise out of the earth. [18]But the holy ones of the Most High shall receive the kingdom and possess the kingdom forever—forever and ever." [19]Then I desired to know the truth concerning the fourth beast, which was different from all the rest, exceedingly terrifying, with its teeth of iron and claws of bronze, and which devoured and broke in pieces, and stamped what was left with its feet; [20]and concerning the

---

Did he accept it from him, or did he not?

Come and hear! One for judging and one for mercy, these are the words of Rabbi Aqiva. [BT Ḥagiga 14a]

Whatever the precise interpretation of this talmudic passage (and I have discussed this at length elsewhere), there may be little doubt that both portrayed Rabbis understood that the Daniel passage was a theophany. "Rabbi Aqiva" perceives two divine figures in heaven, one God the Father and one an apotheosized King David. No wonder that "Rabbi Yose the Galilean" was shocked. In an article in the *Harvard Theological Review*, I have presented the bases for my own conclusion that such was the original meaning of the text as well; see Daniel Boyarin, "Daniel 7, Intertextuality, and the History of Israel's Cult," forthcoming.

ten horns that were on its head, and concerning the other horn, which came up and to make room for which three of them fell out—the horn that had eyes and a mouth that spoke arrogantly, and that seemed greater than the others. [21]As I looked, this horn made war with the holy ones and was prevailing over them, [22]until the Ancient One came; then judgment was given for the holy ones of the Most High, and the time arrived when the holy ones gained possession of the kingdom. [23]This is what he said: "As for the fourth beast, there shall be a fourth kingdom on earth that shall be different from all the other kingdoms; it shall devour the whole earth, and trample it down, and break it to pieces. [24]As for the ten horns, out of this kingdom ten kings shall arise, and another shall arise after them. This one shall be different from the former ones, and shall put down three kings. [25]He shall speak words against the Most High, shall wear out the holy ones of the Most High, and shall attempt to change the sacred seasons and the law; and they shall be given into his power for a time, two times, and half a time. [26]Then the court shall sit in judgment, and his dominion shall be taken away, to be consumed and totally destroyed. [27]The kingship and dominion and the greatness of the kingdoms under the whole heaven shall be given to the people of the holy ones of the Most High; their kingdom shall be an everlasting kingdom, and all dominions shall serve and obey them." [28]Here the account ends. As for me, Daniel, my thoughts greatly terrified me, and my face turned pale; but I kept the matter in my mind.

Those Jews who were Aphrahat's opponents could clearly have retorted, then: "Is a heavenly being or junior God subject to oppression by a Seleucid king who forces him to abandon his Holy Days and his Law for three and a half years? Absurd! The Son of Man must be a symbol for the children of Israel!"

Both sides of this argument are right. As we've just seen, Daniel's vision itself seems to require that we understand "the one like a son of man" as a second divine figure. The angelic decoding of the vision in the end of the chapter seems equally as clearly to interpret "the one like a son of man" as a collective earthly figure, Israel or the righteous of Israel. No wonder the commentators argue. The text itself seems to be a house divided against itself. The answer to this conundrum is that the author of the Book of Daniel, who had Daniel's vision itself before him, wanted to suppress the ancient testimony of a more-than-singular God, using allegory to do so. In this sense, the theological controversy that we think exists between Jews and Christians was already an intra-Jewish controversy long before Jesus.

Ancient Jewish readers might well have reasoned, as the Church Father Aphrahat did, that since the theme of riding on the clouds indicates a divine being in every other instance in the Tanakh (the Jewish name for the Hebrew Bible), we should read this one too as the revelation of God, a second God, as it were. The implication is, of course, that there are two such divine figures in heaven, the old Ancient of Days and the young one like a son of man.[10] Such Jews would have had to explain, then, what it means for this divine figure to be given into the power of the fourth beast for "a time, two times, and a half a time." A descent into hell—or at any rate to the realm of death—for three days would be one fine answer to that question.

The Messiah-Christ existed as a Jewish idea long before the baby Jesus was born in Nazareth. That is, the idea of a second God as viceroy to God the Father is one of the oldest of theological ideas in Israel. Daniel 7 brings into the present a fragment of what is perhaps the most ancient of religious visions of Israel that we can find. Just as seeing an ancient Roman wall built into a modern Roman building enables us to experience ancient Rome alive and functioning in the present, this fragment of ancient lore enabled Jews of the centuries just before Jesus and onward to vivify in the present of their lives this bit of ancient myth.

The rest, as they say, is Gospel. But the point is that these ideas were not new ones at all by the time Jesus appeared on the scene. They are among the earliest ideas about God in the religion of the Israelites, comparable to the ancient relationship between the gods 'El and Baʿal in which "Baʿl comes near in his shining storm cloud. 'El is the transcendent one."[11] 'El, the ancient sky god of all of the Canaanites (his name comes to mean just "God" in biblical Hebrew), was the god of justice, while his younger associate, named Baʿal by most of the Canaanites—but not the Israelites, who called him YHVH—was the god of war. In the biblical religion, in order to form a more perfect monotheism, these two divinities have been merged into one, but not quite seamlessly. The Israelites were a part of that ancient Canaanite community, differentiated to some extent by different ideas about God that they developed through their historical existence, but the idea of a duality within God was not easily escaped, however much certain leaders sought to enforce it. A God that is very far away generates—almost inevitably—a need for a God who is closer; a God who judges us requires almost inevitably a God who will fight for us and defend us (as long as the second God is completely subordinate to the first, the principle of monotheism is not violated).

The unreconstructed relic of Israel's religious past (if not her present as well) that we find in the two-thrones theophany of Daniel 7 was no doubt disturbing to at least some Jews in antiquity, such as the author of Daniel himself in the second century B.C. We know that other Jews adopted wholeheartedly, or simply inherited, the doubleness of Israel's God, the old Ancient of Days and the young human-appearing rider on the clouds. These became the progenitors of the Judaism of Jesus and his followers.

The two-thrones apocalypse in Daniel calls up a very ancient strand in Israel's religion, one in which, it would seem, the 'El-like sky god of justice and the younger rider on the clouds, storm god of war, have not really been merged as they are for most of the Bible.[12] I find it plausible that this highly significant passage is a sign of the religious traditions that gave rise to the notion of a Father divinity and a Son divinity that we find in the Gospels.

Taking the two-throne vision out of the context of Daniel 7 as a whole, we find several crucial elements: (1) there are two thrones; (2) there are two divine figures, one apparently old and one apparently young; (3) the young figure is to be the Redeemer and eternal ruler of the world.[13] It would certainly not be wrong to suggest, I think, that even if the actual notion of the Messiah/Christ is not yet present here, the notion of a divinely appointed divine king over earth is, and that this has great potential for understanding the development of the Messiah/Christ notion in later Judaism (including Christianity, of course). The second-God Redeemer figure thus comes, on my view, out of the earlier history of Israel's religion. Once the messiah had been combined with the younger divine figure that we have found in Daniel 7, then it became natural to ascribe to him also the term "Son of God." The occupant of one throne was an ancient, the occupant of the other a young figure in human form. The older one invests the younger one with His own authority on earth forever and ever, passing the scepter to him. What could be more natural, then, than to adopt the older usage "Son of God," already ascribed to the Messiah in his role as the Davidic king of Israel, and understanding it more literally as the sign of the equal divinity of the Ancient of Days and the Son of Man? Thus the Son of Man became the Son of God, and "Son of God" became the name for Jesus' divine nature—and all without any break with ancient Jewish tradition.

The theology of the Gospels, far from being a radical innovation within Israelite religious tradition, is a highly conservative return to the very most ancient moments within that tradition, moments that had been largely suppressed in the meantime—but not entirely. The identification of the rider on the clouds with the one like a son of man in Daniel provides that name and image of the Son of Man in the Gospels as well. It follows that the ideas about God that we identify as Christian are not innovations but may be deeply connected with some of the most ancient of Israelite ideas about God. These ideas at the very least go back to an entirely plausible (and attested) reading of Daniel 7 and thus to the second century B.C. at the latest. They may even be a whole lot older than that.

One of the most important sources that we have for the most ancient stages of the religion of Israel are some epic texts about the gods of Canaan that were found in an archaeological excavation in a place called Ras Shamra (ancient Ugarit) early in the twentieth century. These epics reveal a very rich ancient Canaanite mythology, especially in the elaborated stories of the gods 'El and Ba'al and their rivals and consorts. While, of course, the Israelite branch of the Canaanite group partly defined itself through the rejection of this mythology, much of the imagery and narrative allusions that we find in the works of the Israelite prophets, the Psalms, and other biblical poetic texts are best illuminated through comparison with these ancient texts. These fragments of reused ancient epic material within the Bible reveal also the existence of an ancient Israelite version of these epics and the mythology that they enact. Yale Divinity School scholar J.J. Collins has helpfully summed up the main points of comparison of Daniel 7 with Canaanite (Ugaritic) representations.[14] As he argues, "What is important is the pattern of relationships,"[15] namely, the fact that in Daniel there are two godlike figures, one old and one young, the younger one comes riding on the clouds, and he receives everlasting dominion.[16] Colpe has noted "the mythographical similarity between the relation of the Ancient of Days and Son of Man on the one side and that of El and Ba'al on the other, which fits into the broader conclusion that older material lives on in the tradition of Israel and Judah."[17]

The most persuasive reconstruction from the evidence

we have shows that in the ancient religion of Israel, 'El was the general Canaanite high divinity while YHVH was the Ba'al-like divinity of a small group of southern Canaanites, the Hebrews, with 'El a very distant absence for these Hebrews. When the groups merged and emerged as Israel,[18] YHVH, the Israelite version of Ba'al, became assimilated to 'El as the high God and their attributes largely merged into one doubled God, with 'El receiving his warlike stormgod characteristics from YHVH.[19] Thus, to restate the point, the ancient 'El and YHVH—a southern Hebrew equivalent in function (within the paradigm of relations between 'El and a young warrior god to the northern Ba'al)[20]—apparently merged at some early point in Israelo-Canaanite history, thus producing a rather tense and unstable monotheism.[21] This merger was not by any means a perfect union. 'El and YHVH had very different and in some ways antithetical functions, and I propose that this left a residue in which some of the characteristics of the young divinity always had the potential to split off again in a hypostasis (or even separate god) of their own.[22] This tension and resultant splitting manifests itself in the traditions behind the Daniel 7 theophany, where we see a new young one, apparently nameless until he comes to be called Jesus—or Enoch.[23] As a medieval rabbinic hymn, still feeling that tension, would have it, YHVH is an "ancient on the day of judgment and a youth on the day of battle."

This merger, if indeed it occurred, must have happened very early on, for the worship of only one God characterizes Israel, at least in aspiration, from the time of Josiah (sixth century B.C.) and the Deuteronomist revolution, if not much earlier. This merger leaves its marks right on the surface of the text, where the 'El-YHVH combination can still be detected in the tensions and doublings of the biblical text, available to be resurrected, as it were, by astute readers of a certain cast of religious mind as a second, young God, or as a part of God, or as a divine person within God (and all of these options have been adopted by perfectly "orthodox," non-Christian Jewish theologians as well as by Christians).[24]

The young God in the original mythic text in Daniel is the figure who will redeem Israel and the world, not an exalted Davidic king.[25] There is, as I have argued, nothing in this vision that suggests or even allows seeing the one like a son of man as an actual human being. Setting aside the internal explanation and just looking at the original vision, however, we do find that this divine figure will be given "the dominion, the glory, the kingdom and all of the peoples, nations, and languages will worship him, and his dominion will be eternal dominion which will not pass and his kingdom which will not be destroyed." This mythic pattern of second God as Redeemer will be crucial, of course, in interpreting the Gospels and the pattern of religion proclaimed there and in which we will have

to try to understand better the relation of this divine Redeemer to the human one, the Davidic Messiah.

The general outlines of a theology of a young God sub-
ordinated to an old God are present in the throne vision
of Daniel 7, however much the author of Daniel labored
to suppress this. In place of notions of 'El and YHVH as
the two Gods of Israel, the pattern of an older god and a
younger one—a god of wise judgment and a god of war
and punishment—has been transferred from older forms
of Israelite/Canaanite religion to new forms. Here, the
older god is now entirely named by the tetragrammaton
YHVH (and his supremacy is not in question), while the
functions of the younger god have been in part taken by
supreme angels or other sorts of divine beings, Redeemer
figures, at least in the "official" religion of the biblical text.
Once YHVH absorbs 'El, the younger god has no name
of his own but presumably is identified at different times
with the archangels or other versions of the Great Angel,
Michael, as well as with Enoch, Christ, and later Meṭaṭron
as well.[26] Some of the ancient guises of the younger god
found in Jewish texts of the Second Temple period and
later, especially "the Little Yahu," Yaho'el," indicate his
extrabiblical identity as YHVH.[27] It is the power of that
myth that explains the continuing life of Jewish binitarianism into Christian Judaism and vitally present in non-
Christian Judaism as well (Little Yahu as a name for the
divine vice-regent; Meṭaṭron appearing as late as the

Byzantine period in a Hebrew Jewish text). There are thus two legacies left us by Daniel 7: it is the ultimate source of "Son of Man" terminology for a heavenly Redeemer figure, and it is also the best evidence we have for the continuation of a very ancient binitarian Israelite theology deep into the Second Temple period. Although these are separate in Daniel (since that text contains no figure explicitly called the Son of Man), it is the not entirely successful suppression of this myth in Daniel and thus its strong association with the "one like a son of man" that will explain the later development of "Son of Man" as a title in the Gospels (as well as some other ancient Jewish religious texts such as the Book of Enoch).

The meaning of the term "Son of Man" and its usage within chapter 7 of Daniel is a bit of very precious evidence—all the more so as it is against the grain of the biblical theology itself—for the continued vitality of worship of an old God and a young God in Israel. This evidence helps clarify the historical ties of that pattern of religion to later forms of Judaism, including both rabbinic Judaism and Christianity.[28] I see it as very much a living part of Israel's religion both before and long after, explaining both the form of Judaism we call Christianity and also much in non-Christian later Judaism as well.[29] If Daniel is the prophecy, the Gospels are the fulfillment.

How the Jews Came to Believe That Jesus Was God

If all the Jews—or even a substantial number—expected that the Messiah would be divine as well as human, then the belief in Jesus as God is not the point of departure on which some new religion came into being but simply another variant (and not a deviant one) of Judaism. As controversial a statement as this may seem, it must first be understood in the context of a broader debate about the origins of the divinity of Jesus. The theological idea that Jesus actually was God, however refined by the later niceties of trinitarian theology, is referred to as a "high Christology," in opposition to "low Christologies" according to which Jesus was essentially an inspired human being, a prophet or teacher, and not God.

"Christology" is the term in Christian theology and the history of Christianity for all of the issues and controversies that make up the story and the doctrine of the Christ. In the fifth century, for instance, the great controversy about whether Jesus had one human nature and one divine nature or one combined divine-human nature was called the "Christological controversy." Many other issues have been discussed and thought about under the rubric of Christology, however. Was Jesus divine from birth or an ordinary human later adopted by God and made divine? How did Jesus effect salvation—through his crucifixion, his teaching, his showing the way for humans to become divine? It has frequently been asserted that low Christologies are "Jewish" ones, while high Christologies have come into Christianity from the Greek thought world. Oddly enough, this position has been taken both by Jewish writers seeking to discredit Christianity as a kind of paganism and by orthodox Christian scholars wishing to distinguish the "new religion" from the old one as far and as quickly as possible. This doubly defensive approach can no longer be maintained.

The question of the origins of high Christology is one that continues to animate a great deal of scholarship on the prehistory of Christianity, or the history of pre-Christianity as attested in the New Testament, for at first glance it would seem to violate the absolute principle of Jewish monotheism. In a recent article, Andrew Chester has helpfully summarized the various positions that are currently held and defended by scholars on this question, which can be divided into four broad schools of thought.[30] According to the first, which has been popular among liberal Protestants for over a century, the idea of the divinity of Christ could only have been a relatively late and "Gentile" development that marks a decisive break with anything that could reasonably be called Jewish. The argument goes that the early Jewish believers in Jesus believed in him as an inspired teacher, perhaps a prophet, perhaps the Messiah but only in the human sense. It was only later on, this view would hold, after the majority of

Christians were no longer Jews, that the idea of Jesus as God came in, possibly under the sway of the "pagan" ideas of many of the new Christian converts.

A second approach, currently enjoying ascendance especially among New Testament scholars, sees the earliest versions of high Christology as emerging within a Jewish religious context.[31] I submit that it is possible to understand the Gospel only if both Jesus and the Jews around him held to a high Christology whereby the claim to Messiahship was also a claim to being a divine man.* Were it not the case, we would be very hard-pressed to understand the extremely hostile reaction to Jesus on the part of Jewish leaders who did not accept his claim. Controversy

---

* Adela Yarbro Collins has recently distinguished two senses of "divinity": "One is functional. The 'one like a son of man' in Daniel 7:13–14, 'that Son of Man' in the Similitudes of Enoch, and Jesus in some Synoptic passages are divine in this sense when they exercise (or are anticipated as exercising) divine activities like ruling over a universal kingdom, sitting on a heavenly throne, judging human beings in the end-time or traveling on the clouds, a typically divine mode of transport. The other sense is ontological." Adela Yarbro Collins, " 'How on Earth Did Jesus Become God': A Reply," in *Israel's God and Rebecca's Children: Christology and Community in Early Judaism and Christianity: Essays in Honor of Larry W. Hurtado and Alan F. Segal*, ed. David B. Capes et al. (Waco, TX: Baylor University Press, 2007), 57. It is that former sense to which I refer throughout this book, as I believe that the very distinction between "functional" and "ontological" is a product of later Greek reflection on the Gospels. In this context, see the ever-sensible and ever-helpful Paula Fredriksen, "Mandatory Retirement: Ideas in the Study of Christian Origins Whose Time Has Come to Go," in *Israel's God and Rebecca's Children*, 35–38. (I am grateful to Adela Yarbro Collins for this last reference.)

among Jews was hardly a new thing; for a controversy to lead to a crucifixion, it must have been a doozy. A Jew claiming that he was God, that he was the divine Son of Man whom the Jews had been expecting and, moreover, not being laughed out of the village for this claim, would have been such a doozy.

The Blasphemy of the Son of Man

The reasons that many Jews came to believe that Jesus was divine was because they were already expecting that the Messiah/Christ would be a god-man. *This expectation was part and parcel of Jewish tradition.* The Jews had learned this by careful reading of the Book of Daniel and understanding its visions and revelations as a prophecy of what would happen at the end of time. In that book, as we have just seen, the young divine figure is given sovereignty and made ruler of the world forever. I want to show that Jesus saw himself as the divine Son of Man, and I will do so by explaining a couple of difficult passages in the second chapter of the Gospel of Mark.

The Son of Man has been afforded glory, sovereignty, and dominion over all the sublunary world, as we saw in Daniel 7 above: "[27]The kingship and dominion and the greatness of the kingdoms *under the whole heaven* shall be given to the people of the holy ones of the Most High; their kingdom shall be an everlasting kingdom, and all dominions shall serve and obey them." While this verse comes from an interpretative framework within the chapter that seeks to demythologize the narrative of the Son of Man, such effort could not withstand the power of the verses earlier in the chapter in which the divinity of the Son of Man is so clearly marked.

In Mark 2:5–10 we read the following:

[5]And when Jesus saw their faith, he said to the paralytic, "My son, your sins are forgiven." [6]Now some of the scribes were sitting there, questioning in their hearts, [7]"Why does this man speak thus? It is blasphemy! Who can forgive sins except the one God?"[32] [8]And immediately Jesus, perceiving in his spirit that they thus questioned within themselves, said to them, "Why do you question thus in your hearts? [9]Which is easier, to say to the paralytic, 'Your sins are forgiven,' or to say, 'Rise, take up your pallet and walk'? [10]But that you may know that the Son of man has authority on earth to forgive sins"—he said to the paralytic . . .

"But that you may know that the Son of man has authority on earth to forgive sins." The Son of Man has authority (obviously delegated by God) to do God's work of the forgiving of sins on earth. This claim is derived from Daniel 7:14, in which we read that the one like a son of man has been given "authority, glory, kingship"—indeed, an "authority that is eternal that will not pass away." The term that we conventionally translate as "authority" in its New Testament contexts, ἐξουσία, is exactly the same term that translates the Aramaic שלטן in the Septuagint, namely, "sovereignty" or "dominion." That is, what Jesus is claiming for the Son of Man is exactly what has been granted to the one like a son of man in Daniel; Jesus rests his claim on the ancient text quite directly.[33] According to this tradition, then, Jesus claims to be the Son of Man to whom divine authority on earth "under the heavens" (Daniel 7:27) has been delegated.[34] The sovereign, moreover, is the one who has the power to declare exceptions to the Law.

The objection of the Scribes, calling Jesus' act of forgiveness "blasphemy," is predicated on their assumption that Jesus is claiming divinity through this action; hence their emphasis that only the *one* God may forgive sins, to which Jesus answers in kind: the second divine figure of Daniel 7, the one like a son of man, is authorized to act as and for God. This constitutes a direct declaration of a doubleness of the Godhead, which is, of course, later on the very hallmark of Christian theology. Throughout the Gospel, whenever Jesus claims ἐξουσία to perform that which appears to be the prerogative of the divinity, it is that very ἐξουσία of the Son of Man that is being claimed, which is to say, a scriptural authority based on a very close reading of Daniel 7.[35] We see now why the later Rabbis, in naming this very ancient religious view a heresy, refer to it as "two powers in heaven."

"The Son of Man Is Lord Even of the Sabbath"

The question of how to read Daniel 7 was very much on the minds of Jews of the period, and not only those who became followers of Jesus. Mark, quite directly and intentionally, is offering us a close reading of Daniel. In this light, we can begin to interpret one of the most puzzling and pivotal "Son of Man" statements in the Gospel. I place these texts in an entirely different context from the one in which they are usually read; in this new context, certain clues become much more vivid and telling. It's a question of looking at the text in a new and different way, which in turn reveals connections that help sketch an entirely different picture of what's going on—or better put, what was at stake for the evangelist and his hearers. This interpretation of Mark 2:10 as being a close reading of Daniel 7:14 enables me to begin to understand anew the other puzzling Son of Man statement in Mark 2, known as the incident of the plucking of grain on the Sabbath. In this story, Jesus' disciples are discovered plucking grain and eating it as they walk on the Sabbath by some Pharisees who challenge Jesus as to this seemingly insouciant or arrogant violation of the Sabbath. Jesus defends them vigorously.

This passage helps us understand how it was that Jesus saw himself (or is portrayed as seeing himself) both as the divine Redeemer and as the Davidic Messiah whom the Jews were expecting:

> [23]One sabbath he was going through the grainfields; and as they made their way his disciples began to pluck heads of grain. [24]And the Pharisees said to him, "Look, why are they doing what is not lawful on the sabbath?" [25]And he said to them, "Have you never read what David did, when he was in need and was hungry, he and those who were with him: [26]how he entered the house of God, when Abiathar was high priest, and ate the bread of the Presence, which it is not lawful for any but the priests to eat, and also gave it to those who were with him?" [27]And he said to them, "The sabbath was made for man, not man for the sabbath; [28]so the Son of man is lord even of the sabbath."

There are several well-known problems attending on this passage, which (as is Mark 7, which I will presently treat) is of enormous importance for reconstructing Jewish religious history.[36] The major issues are the reason for the disciples plucking on the Sabbath; the nature and meaning of Jesus' reply invoking the analogy of David; the connection between that reply and vv. 27–28, in which the Son of Man is Lord of the Sabbath, and the Sabbath is made for man; and the meaning and connection between those verses.[37] Jesus seems to be giving too many justifications of the disciples' behavior; is the defense based on an ancient halakhic principle that the Sabbath may be violated for human welfare, or does it have something to do with Jesus' messianic status? Many scholars have "solved" these problems by assuming that the text has been interpolated. This explanation, while in itself unsatisfactory, points up the tension in the text between ancient halakhic (legal) controversy (which there certainly is here) and radical apocalyptic transformation in the words of Jesus (which I believe is also here). What convinces me that there is genuine memory of halakhic controversy here is the fact that the elements of Jesus' arguments are found later within the traditions of the Rabbis.*

---

* "The Rabbis" is a designation for the leaders of a group of Jewish teachers who produced the Mishna, the midrashim, and the two Talmuds, Palestinian and Babylonian. They flourished from the second through the seventh centuries A.D. in Palestine and Babylonia and were eventually accepted as the authoritative transmitters of Judaism. The authorities cited in this passage are all second-century Palestinians (*tannaim*), so even if the attributions are genuine, the text is later than the Gospels. Although the rabbinic parallel does illumine some aspects of Jesus' statement— namely, its scriptural basis—what is more important is that the Gospel attests to the antiquity of a rabbinic idea. What we see here is convergence (despite some vitally important differences) between two sets of Jewish traditions about the Sabbath, both of which permitted at least some healing on the Sabbath based in part on the same reasoning, namely, that the Sabbath was given to benefit those who keep it, not that the people are there to serve the Sabbath.

Here is the crucial text for our purposes:

Rabbi Ishmael and Rabbi El'azar the son of Azariah and Rabbi Akiva were walking on the way and
Levi Hassaddar and Rabbi Ishmael the son of Rabbi
El'azar the son of Azariah were walking behind
them. And the question arose among them: *"From
whence do we know that the saving of a life supersedes
the Sabbath?"*

Rabbi Ishmael answered: Behold it says: "If a
thief is caught breaking in and is struck so that he
dies, the defender is not guilty of bloodshed; ³but if
it happens after sunrise, he is guilty of bloodshed"
[Exodus 22:2–3]. And this is true even if we are not
sure whether he came to kill or only to steal. Now
the reasoning is from the light to the heavy: Just as
the killing of a person which pollutes the Land and
pushes the divine presence away supersedes the
Sabbath (in such a case of one caught at night breaking and entering), even more so the saving of a life!"

Rabbi El'azar spoke up with a different answer:
"Just as circumcision which [saves] only one member of a person supersedes the Sabbath, the entire
body even more so!" . . .

Rabbi Akiva says: "If murder supersedes the
Temple worship which supersedes the Sabbath, saving a life even more so!"

Rabbi Yose Hagelili says: "When it says 'But keep

my Sabbaths,' the word 'but' makes a distinction: There are Sabbaths that you push aside and those that you keep [i.e., when human life is at stake, this supersedes the Sabbath]."

Rabbi Shim'on the son of Menasya says: "Behold it says: Keep the Sabbath because it is holy to *you*; to *you* the Sabbath is delivered and not you to the Sabbath." Rabbi Natan says: "It says: And the Children of Israel kept the Sabbath to keep the Sabbath for their generations. Profane one Sabbath for him [the sick person] in order that he may keep many Sabbaths!" (Mekhilta, Tractate Sabbath, 1)[38]

In seeking to distinguish the radically new and un-Jewish in Jesus' preaching, Christian writers have frequently read his statement that the Sabbath was made for man and not man for the Sabbath both as indicating total opposition to the keeping of the Sabbath laws at all and as initiating a religion of love and not one of casuistry. In this text, however, we see that the Rabbis themselves held views about the Sabbath that were closely related to Jesus' own (more expansive, to be sure) views, certainly not in direct contradiction of them. The thematic similarities between some of these arguments and Jesus' arguments in the Gospel are striking. This parallel gets even stronger when we consider one further argument that we find in Matthew 12 but not in Mark: "Or have you not read in

the law how on the sabbath the priests in the temple profane the sabbath and are guiltless? I tell you something
greater than the Temple is here," thus providing a parallel
to Rabbi Akiva's argument from the Temple as well.[39]

Jesus may very well have been in controversy with ancient Pharisees who had not yet articulated the principle
that saving a life supersedes the Sabbath. As my colleague
Aharon Shemesh points out, such was the opinion of the
Jews of the Dead Sea Community.[40] Jesus' teaching in this
regard, however, is hardly in opposition to the teaching of
the later *tannaim*, who possibly did learn it from Jesus but
probably did not. What is distinctive to the Jesus of the
Gospels is, I think, the further apocalyptic extension of
these principles, namely, the Son of Man statement—the
statement that the Son of Man, the divine Messiah, is now
lord of the Sabbath.

It is this too that explains the one probable and potentially huge difference between the saying of the Rabbis and
that of the evangelist (or Jesus). The rabbinic interpretations, and their halakha, tend strongly in the direction of
allowing the violation of the Sabbath by a Jew to save another Jew, while the setting of Jesus' saying and its consequence seem (but not inescapably) to indicate that any
human might be saved on the Sabbath. If it is the case, as it
seems, that the Rabbis' law applies only to Jews, Jesus' extension of it is a product of the radical apocalyptic moment
within which the Gospel of Mark is written, a moment

in which the Torah was not rejected but expanded and "fulfilled"—to use Matthean terminology—a moment in which the Son of Man was revealed and claimed his full authority.[41] The Son of Man, according to Daniel, was indeed given jurisdiction over all of the nations, and I would suggest gingerly that this explains the extension of the Sabbath (and thus Sabbath healing) to them. Here in Mark we find a Jesus who is fulfilling the Torah, not abrogating it.

The Gospels are testimony to the antiquity of themes and controversies that later appear in rabbinic literature. Since there is little reason to believe that the Rabbis actually read the Gospels, it follows that we have independent witnesses to these controversies. The arguments from David's violation of the Torah, from the assertion that the Sabbath was made for the human being, and from the service in the Temple constituting a permitted violation of the Sabbath (the latter found in Matthew and not in Mark) are all mobilized in rabbinic literature in order to justify saving life on the Sabbath (including, no doubt, salvation from starvation), with only the important proviso that it must be necessary for the healing to be done on the Sabbath, that is, the condition is life-threatening, or might be if not treated. This concatenation can hardly be coincidental; some very early version of a controversy of the permission to heal on Sabbath is to be found in this passage.[42] Were we to remain at this level of interpretation, we would find a not particularly radical, even strangely "rabbinic" Jesus fighting against some rigorists whom he identifies as Pharisees. However, this approach leaves too much in the text unexplained. It doesn't explain at all the argument from David's having fed himself and his followers on forbidden bread. We will see presently how taking that textual moment seriously will reveal another dimension of the Markan theology of Jesus (Christology).[43]

In short, my suggestion is that a set of controversy arguments in favor of allowing violation of the Sabbath for healing (now an accepted practice) has been overlaid with and radicalized by a further apocalyptic moment suggested by the very connection with David's behavior. The David story itself can go either way. Just as the Rabbis chose to emphasize David's hunger and thus the lifesaving aspect of the story, justifying other breaches of the law if a life can be saved (Palestinian Talmud Yoma 8:6, 45:b), so did Matthew; Mark, by contrast, understanding the story as being about the special privileges of the Messiah, pushed it in the direction that he did. On this account, the reason for the absence of v. 27 in Matthew (and Luke) is that Mark's messianic theology was a bit too radical for the later evangelists.

I think that the problems of this sequence of verses are best unraveled if we take seriously its context following Mark 2:10, as I have just discussed. If Jesus (the Markan Jesus, or the Jesus of these passages) proclaims himself as the Son of Man who has ἐξουσία by virtue of Daniel 7:14, then it is entirely plausible that he would claim sovereignty over the Sabbath as well. Extending the clearly controversial notion that healing is permitted on the Sabbath by virtue of various biblical precedents and arguments, Jesus makes a much more radical claim: not only does the Torah authorize healing of the deathly sick on the Sabbath, but the Messiah himself, the Son of Man, is given sovereignty to decide how to further extend and interpret the Sabbath law. This is, I suggest, primarily motivated by the fact that it is David who violates the Law to feed his minions, so Jesus— the new David, the Son of Man—may do so to feed his minyan.[44] The point is surely not—as certain interpreters give it—that David violated the Law and God did not protest, so therefore the Law is invalid and anyone may violate it. Rather, it is that David, the type of the Messiah, enjoyed sovereignty to set aside parts of the Law, and so too does Jesus, the new David, the Messiah. This is not an attack on the Law or on alleged pharisaic legalism but an apocalyptic declaration of a new moment in history in which a new Lord, the Son of Man, has been appointed over the Law.

Paying attention to the Danielic allusion implicit in every use of the phrase "Son of Man," one can see that in all those situations the Markan Jesus is making precisely the same kind of claim on the basis of the authority delegated to the Son of Man in Daniel as he does in Mark 2:10.[45] This enables me to propose a solution to the sequence of vv. 27–28. One objection could be that the

Sabbath is not "under the heavens" but in heaven and thus not susceptible to the transfer of authority from the Ancient of Days to the one like a son of man. This objection is entirely answered by the statement that the Sabbath was made for the human being; consequently the Son of Man, having been given dominion in the human realm, is the Lord of the Sabbath.[46] It is actually a necessary part of the argument that the Son of Man is Lord of the Sabbath, for if the Sabbath is (as one might very well claim on the basis of Genesis 1) in heaven, then the claim that the Son of Man, who has sovereignty only on earth, can abrogate its provisions would be very weak. I think that this explanation of the connection between vv. 27 and 28 answers many interpretative conundrums that arise when 27 is read as a weak humanistic statement, something like "The Sabbath was made for man, so do whatever you want."[47] In my view, in contrast, what may have been a traditional Jewish saying to justify breaking the Sabbath to preserve life is, in the hands of Mark's Jesus, the justification for a *messianic* abrogation of the Sabbath.[48] This interpretation has the virtue, I think, of solving two major interpretative sticking points in the text: the unity of the two answers of Jesus (both are references to his messianic status) and the subordination of "So the Son of Man is lord even of the Sabbath."[49]

The halakhic arguments in Jesus' mouth here and in chapter 7 are too well formed and well attested historically to be ignored; Jesus, or Mark, certainly knew his way around a halakhic argument.[50] They are not a relic but represent, I believe, actual contests from the first century, and as such, they provide precious evidence that such halakhic discourse and reasoning was extant already then. But that is not all there is here, of course. There are two elements that mark off the Gospel mobilization of these arguments from a purely halakhic controversy. The first is that in both cases, Jesus uses the argument itself and the halakha itself as a sign of an ethical reading, a kind of parable (called such explicitly in chapter 7); the second and most exciting is that the apocalyptic element of the Son of Man is introduced here, as in the story of the paralytic, to bring home the messianic nature, the divine-human nature, of the sovereignty of Jesus as the Son of Man now on earth. The comparison to David is, of course, very pointed and does suggest that the Redeemer of Daniel 7:13–14 is indeed understood as the messianic king, son of David. I would find here, therefore, clear evidence of identification of the Davidic Messiah with the Son of Man, an identification that clearly does not require a human genealogical connection between the two, for the Son of Man is a figure entirely heavenly who becomes a human being.[51] There were other ancient Jews from around the time of the earliest Gospel writings who also read Daniel 7 in the way that I am suggesting Jesus did. On this reading, Mark's saying about the Son of Man being Lord of the Sabbath is precisely a radical eschatological move, but not one that is constituted by a step outside of the broad community of Israelites or even Jews. If Daniel's vision is now being fulfilled through the person of Jesus as the incarnation of the Son of Man, some radical change is exactly what would be expected during the end times. The sovereign, we are told by modern political theorists, is the one who can make exceptions to the law when judged necessary or appropriate. It is exactly for such judgments that the Son of Man was given sovereignty. The sovereignty is expressed by extending the permission granted to Jews to violate the Sabbath to save the lives of other Sabbath observers by Jesus the Messiah to include all humans. This eschatological move is one that many Jews would have rejected not because they did not believe that the Son of Man is Lord of the Sabbath but because they did not believe that Jesus was the Son of Man.

I would argue that this divine figure to whom authority has been delegated is a Redeemer king, as the Daniel passage clearly states.[52] Thus he stands ripe for identification with the Davidic Messiah, as he is in the Gospel and also in non-Christian contemporary Jewish literature such as Enoch and Fourth Ezra. The usage of "Son of Man" in the Gospels joins up with the evidence of such usage from these other ancient Jewish texts to lead us to consider this term used in this way (and, more important, the concept of a second divinity implied by it) as the common coin—which I emphasize does not mean universal or uncontested—of Judaism already before Jesus.

2

The Son of Man in First Enoch and Fourth Ezra: Other Jewish Messiahs of the First Century

THE JESUS FOLK were not alone on the Jewish scene. Other Jews had been imagining various human figures as achieving the status of divinity and sitting next to God or even in God's place on the divine throne. At about the time of the Book of Daniel, Ezekiel the Tragedian, an Alexandrian Jew, wrote:

> *I had a vision of a great throne on the top of Mount*
> *   Sinai*
> *and it reached till the folds of heaven.*
> *A noble man was sitting on it,*
> *with a crown and a large sceptre in his*
> *left hand. He beckoned to me with his right hand,*
> *so I approached and stood before the throne.*

He gave me the sceptre and instructed me to sit
on the great throne. Then he gave me the royal crown
and got up, from the throne.[1]

Here we have the crucial image of the divine throne
and the emplacement of a second figure on the throne
alongside of or even in place of the Ancient One. Within
the context of Second Temple Judaism, "if we find a figure distinguishable from God seated on God's throne itself, we should see that as one of Judaism's most potent
theological symbolical means of including such a figure in
the unique divine identity."[2] Following this principle, we
see that in this text Moses has become God. Not such an
impossible thought, then, for a Jew, even one who lived
long before Jesus. If Moses could be God in one version
of a Jewish religious imagination, then why not Jesus in
another?

Jews at the same time of Jesus had been waiting for a
Messiah who was both human and divine and who was
the Son of Man, an idea they derived from the passage
from Daniel 7. Almost the entire story of the Christ—
with important variations to be sure—is found as well in
the religious ideas of some Jews who didn't even know
about Jesus. Jesus for his followers fulfilled the idea of
the Christ; the Christ was not invented to explain Jesus'
life and death. Versions of this narrative, the Son of Man
story (the story that is later named Christology), were

widespread among Jews before the advent of Jesus; Jesus entered into a role that existed prior to his birth, and this is why so many Jews were prepared to accept him as the Christ, as the Messiah, Son of Man. This way of looking at things is quite opposite to a scholarly tradition that assumes that Jesus came first and that Christology was created after the fact in order to explain his amazing career. The job description—Required: one Christ, will be divine, will be called Son of Man, will be sovereign and savior of the Jews and the world—was there already and Jesus fit (or did not according to other Jews) the bill. The job description was not a put-up job tailored to fit Jesus!

The single most exciting document for understanding this aspect of the early history of the Christ idea is to be found in a book known as the Similitudes (or Parables) of Enoch. This marvelous text (which seems to have been produced at just about the same time as the earliest of the Gospels) shows that there were other Palestinian Jews who expected a Redeemer known as the Son of Man, who would be a divine figure embodied in an exalted human. Because it is unconnected with the Gospels in any direct way, this text is thus an independent witness to the presence of this religious idea among Palestinian Jews of the time and not only among the Jewish groups within which Jesus was active.

The Similitudes of Enoch

The Book of Enoch is a key part of the Bible of the Ethiopian Orthodox Church; it does not appear in Western Bibles, whether Jewish, Catholic, Orthodox, or Protestant. The Book of Enoch contains five sub-books: the Book of the Watchers, the Similitudes of Enoch, the Astronomical Book, the Animal Apocalypse, and the Epistle of Enoch. These books, all purporting to have been written by the antediluvian Enoch, were separate works gathered together at some point, probably during the late first century A.D. Fragments of them have been found at Qumran (among the Dead Sea Scrolls), except for the Similitudes, and fragments are known from various Greek sources as well. Present opinion is almost entirely solid that the Book of the Watchers is the oldest bit of Enoch (third century B.C.) and the Similitudes, our present concern, the youngest, dating from the mid-first century A.D. All of the pieces are couched as visions beheld or shown to that ancient sage Enoch, and thus the text as a whole is an apocalypse, a revelation, similar to the Book of Daniel or the canonical New Testament book of Revelation.

The Similitudes and the Gospels

In the Similitudes of Enoch, a Jewish writer of sometime in the first century A.D.[3] makes extensive use of the term "Son of Man" to refer to a particular divine-human Redeemer figure eventually incarnated in the figure of Enoch, thus exhibiting many of the elements that make up the Christ story.[4] Enoch's "Son of Man" is the descendant in the tradition of Daniel's "one like a son of man."[5] In the Similitudes of Enoch, Chapter 46, we are provided with the following vision of Enoch the visionary speaker:

> There I saw one who had a head of days, and his head was like white wool.[6] And with him was another, whose face was like the appearance of a man; and his face was full of graciousness like one of the holy angels. And I asked the angel of peace, who went with me and showed me all the hidden things, about that son of man—who he was and whence he was [and] why he went with the Head of Days. And he answered me and said to me, "This is the son of man who has righteousness. . . ."

In the Enoch text, just as in Daniel and in almost the same wording, there are two divine figures, one again who is ancient and one who has the appearance of a man, the appearance of a "son of man," a young man, or so it seems in contrast to the Ancient One. It is clear that Enoch knows exactly who the "head of days" is, but he wonders who Son of Man is. There is dramatic irony here. Although Enoch does not know who the Son of Man is, we do—the one who in Daniel comes with the Ancient of Days of the snowy

beard and two thrones as well. By the end of the Similitudes of Enoch, as we shall see below, Enoch will have become that Son of Man, much as Jesus does in the Gospels.

This book provides us with our most explicit evidence
that the Son of Man as a divine-human Redeemer arose by
Jesus' time from reading the Book of Daniel. Chapter 46
of the book actually provides an exciting demonstration
of the process of that reading. We can see there how the
chapter of Daniel has been used in the making of a new
"myth," in the case of the Similitudes; for other Jews, no
doubt, the myth of the Messiah formed in the same way.
The interpretative process that we observe in this case is
an early form of the type of Jewish biblical interpretation
later known as midrash.[7]* Strikingly, however, Enoch's
angel contradicts Daniel's. While Daniel's angel explains
that the Son of Man is a symbol for the holy ones of Israel
(the Maccabean martyrs), Enoch's angel explains the Son

---

* Although a whole library could (and has been) written on midrash, for
the present purposes it will be sufficient to define it as a mode of biblical
reading that brings disparate passages and verses together in the elabora-
tion of new narratives. It is something like the old game of anagrams in
which the players look at words or texts and seek to form new words
and texts out of the letters that are there. The rabbis who produced the
midrashic way of reading considered the Bible one enormous signifying
system, any part of which could be taken as commenting on or supple-
menting any other part. They were thus able to make new stories out of
fragments of older ones (from the Bible itself), via a kind of anagrams writ
large; the new stories, which build closely on the biblical narratives but
expand and modify them as well, were considered the equals of the biblical stories themselves.

of Man as a righteous divine figure. As we have seen in chapter 1 of this book, this seems to have been the original meaning of the vision, a meaning the author/redactor of the Book of Daniel sought to suppress by having the angel interpret the Son of Man allegorically. What we learn from this is that there was controversy among Jews about the Son of Man long before the Gospels were written. Some Jews accepted and some rejected the idea of a divine Messiah. The Similitudes are evidence for the tradition of interpretation of the Son of Man as such a divine person, the tradition that fed into the Jesus movement as well. It is only centuries later, of course, that this difference in belief would become the marker and touchstone of the difference between two religions.

Son of Man speculation and expectation seem, then, to have been a widespread form of Jewish belief at the end of the Second Temple period. The Similitudes seem to have been not the product of an isolated sect but part of a more general Jewish world of thought and writing.[8] Jesus' God-man Messiahship was just what the Jews ordered, even if many didn't think he fit the bill (and many others outside of Palestine, at least, never heard of him).

In the Book of Enoch, this figure is a part of God; as a second or junior divinity, he may even be considered a Son alongside the Ancient of Days, whom we might begin to think of as the Father. Although the Messiah designation appears elsewhere also, it is in Enoch 48 that the similarities to the Gospel ideas about Jesus are most pronounced. Here is this riveting passage in its entirety:

> ¹*In that place I saw the spring of righteousness, and it was inexhaustible, and many springs of wisdom surrounded it.*
>
> *And all the thirsty drank from them and were filled with wisdom;*
>
> *and their dwelling places were with the righteous and the holy and the chosen.*
>
> ²*And in that hour that son of man was named in the presence of the Lord of Spirits,*
>
> *and his name, before the Head of Days.*
>
> ³*Even before the sun and the constellations were created,*
>
> *before the stars of heaven were made,*
>
> *his name was named before the Lord of Spirits.*
>
> ⁴*He will be a staff for the righteous,*
>
> *that they may lean on him and not fall;*
>
> *And he will be the light of the nations,*
>
> *and he will be a hope for those who grieve in their hearts.*
>
> ⁵*All who dwell on the earth will fall down and worship before him,*
>
> *and they will glorify and bless and sing hymns to the name of the Lord of Spirits.*
>
> ⁶*For this reason he was chosen and hidden in his presence before the world was created and forever.*

[7]And the wisdom of the Lord of Spirits has revealed
     him to the holy and the righteous;
for he has preserved the portion of the righteous.
For they have hated and despised this age of
     unrighteousness;
Indeed, all its deeds and its ways they have hated in
     the name of the Lord of Spirits.
For in his name they are saved.
and he is the vindicator of their lives.
[8]In those days, downcast will be the faces of the kings of
     the earth,
and the strong who possess the earth, because of the
     deeds of their hands.
For on the day of their tribulation and distress they
     will not save themselves;
[9]and into the hands of my chosen ones I shall throw them.
As straw in the fire and as lead in the water,
thus they will burn before the face of the holy,
and they will sink before the face of the righteous;
and no trace of them will be found.
[10]And on the day of their distress there will be rest on
     the earth,
and before them they will fall and not rise,
and there will be no one to take them with his hand
     and raise them.
For they have denied the Lord of Spirits and his
     Anointed One.
Blessed be the name of the Lord of Spirits.[9]

This piece of beautiful religious poetry forms an absolutely pivotal text for illuminating the Christology of the Gospels—as well as for demonstrating the essential Jewishness of that phenomenon. First of all, we find here the doctrine of the preexistence of the Son of Man. He was named even before the universe came into being. Second, the Son of Man will be worshipped on earth: "All who dwell on the earth will fall down and worship before him, and they will glorify and bless and sing hymns to the name of the Lord of Spirits." Third, and perhaps most important of all, in v. 10 he is named as the Anointed One, which is precisely the Messiah (Hebrew *mashiah*) or Christ (Greek *Christos*). It seems quite clear, therefore, that many of the religious ideas that were held about the Christ who was identified as Jesus were already present in the Judaism from which both the Enoch circle and the circles around Jesus emerged.

An equally exciting revelation comes in chapter 69 of the Similitudes, where we read about the final judgment:

> [26]*And they had great joy,*
> *and they blessed and glorified and exalted,*
> *because the name of that son of man had been revealed to them.*
> [27]And he sat on the throne of glory

and the whole judgment was given to the son of
    man,
and he will make sinners vanish and perish from the
    face of the earth.
[28]*And those who led the world astray will be bound in*
    chains,
and in the assembly place of their destruction they will
    be confined;
and all their works will vanish from the race of the
    earth,
[29]And from then on there will be nothing that is
    corruptible;
for that son of man has appeared,
And he has sat down on the throne of his
    glory,
and all evil will vanish from his presence.
And the word of the son of man will go forth
And will prevail in the presence of the Lord of
    Spirits.[10]

Here the Son of Man is clearly occupying his throne
of glory, seated, perhaps, at the right hand of the Ancient
of Days. It is hard to escape the conclusion that the Son of
Man is in fact a second person, as it were, of God. And all
of the functions assigned to the divine figure called "one
like a son of man" in Daniel 7 are given to this Son of Man,
who is also called, as we have seen, the Christ.

And Enoch Was with God: The Apotheosis of Enoch

One of the most striking aspects of the doctrine of Christ is the combination in one figure of man and God. Even this radical idea, however, is not unique among Jews to followers of Jesus. We find it in the Similitudes as well. In the main body of the Similitudes, Enoch is *not* the Son of Man. This is emphatically the case, since in chapter 46 and throughout the main body of the text, he is the one who sees the Son of Man and to whom is revealed the description of the Son of Man as the eschatological Redeemer and Messiah; therefore Enoch cannot be identical with him.[11] In the end, however, in chapters 70 and 71, Enoch becomes the Son of Man—he becomes God.[12]

In these chapters we have a remarkable exaltation scene. In chapter 70, we are told of Enoch in the third person: "And it came to pass after this [that], while he was living, his name was lifted from those who dwell upon the dry ground to the presence of the Son of Man *and* to the presence of the Lord of Spirits. And he was lifted on the chariots of the spirit, and *his* name vanished among them." But then, without pause, the text shifts into the first person, and we are told, "And from that day I was not *counted* among them." We have here a midrashic expansion of the famous Enoch verse from Genesis that "Enoch walked with God and he was not": that is, an instance of apotheosis, of a special human becoming divine. As Moshe Idel, the world-renowned scholar of Kabbalah, has remarked:

> Various important developments in the history of Jewish mysticism [are to be explained as] an ongoing competition and synthesis between two main vectors: the apotheotic and the theophanic. The former represents the impulses of a few elite individuals to transcend the human mortal situation through a process of theosis, by ascending on high, to be transformed into a more lasting entity, an angel or God. In contrast to this upward aspiration is the theophanic vector, which stands for the revelation of the divine in a direct manner or via mediating hierarchies.[13]

This very competition is being worked out in the pages of the Enochic Similitudes; moreover, a crucial synthesis is taking place, a synthesis of apotheotic and theophanic traditions that is key to the religious background of the Gospels as well. In Enoch here, as in the nearly contemporary Gospels, we find a powerful connection or synthesis between the idea of God made manifest to men by appearing on earth as a man (theophany) and of a man being raised to the level of divinity (apotheosis).

In these final chapters of the Similitudes, Enoch is shown all of the secrets of the universe and brought to the house of the archangels, with the Ancient of Days among them. In chapter 71, the Ancient of Days comes to Enoch and declares, "You are the Son of Man who was born to righteousness, and righteousness remains over you, and the righteousness of the Ancient of Days will not leave you." Enoch has been exalted and been fused with the Son of Man, the preexistent divine Redeemer and heavenly Messiah whom we have already met.[14]

Enoch Becomes the Son of Man

Notwithstanding later theological niceties, the Gospels also comprise a story of a God who becomes man (theophany) and another of a man who becomes God (apotheosis). That is, we can still observe within the Gospel (especially in Mark, which has no miraculous birth story, and also even in Paul) the remnants of a version of Christology in which Jesus was born a man but became God at his baptism. This idea, later named the heresy of adoptionism (God adopting Jesus as his Son), was not quite stamped out until the Middle Ages. Seeing the doubleness of the narrative of the Son of Man in the Enoch book thus helps us understand the doubleness of the story of Jesus in the Gospels as well. It helps us make sense of the multiple acts of the Christ story: his birth as God, his becoming of God at his baptism, his death and resurrection as a living human once again, teaching on earth, and then his exaltation to the right hand of God for eternity. It is almost as if two stories have been brought together into one plot: one story of a God who became man, came down to earth, and returned home, and a second story of a man who became God and then ascended on high.

Looking at Enoch in detail will teach us much about the religion and religious history of these Jews who believed that a man became God (or that God became a man). The roots of Enoch's apotheosis seem to go back very far in the ancient Near East. I hope to uncover the outlines of a fateful moment in Jewish religious history, the one in which the doctrine of the Messiah as an incarnate divine person and as an exalted human is formed.[15] It is good to remember here that the idea of the Messiah originally centered around an ordinary, human king of the House of David who would restore that longed-for monarchy, while the idea of a divine Redeemer developed separately. It is around the time of Jesus (or actually somewhat earlier) that these two ideas are combined into the concept of a divine Messiah. The best evidence for this is that in the Similitudes, we find the same combination of religious notions that we find in the contemporaneous Gospels.

The preexistence of the Son of Man is quite explicitly brought out in the Similitudes at 48:2–3: "And at that hour that Son of Man was named in the presence of the Lord of Spirits, and his name before the Head of Days.

Even before the sun and the constellations were created, before the stars of heaven were made, his name was named before the Lord of Spirits." This is the same chapter in which he is named as the Messiah as well. Moreover, in the verses that continue from this one, he is indicated as the Redeemer and also one to whom worship is due: "He will be a staff for the righteous, that they may lean on him and not fall; And he will be the light of the nations, and he will be a hope for those who grieve in their hearts. All who dwell on the earth will fall down and worship before him, and they will glorify and bless and sing hymns to the name of the Lord of Spirits. For this [reason] he was chosen and hidden in his presence before the world was created and forever" (vv. 4–6). And finally: "For in his name [the righteous] are saved, and he is the vindicator of their lives" (v. 7).

This is not precisely the same sort of tradition as the one that involves the ascension of a human figure to the position of preexistent heavenly Redeemer, however; the two themes seem almost to contradict each other. In chapter 46 and its sequels, the Son of Man is divine and Enoch a wise seer who has been afforded remarkable visions; in chapters 70–71, Enoch himself has been identified as divine. This is a version of the apotheosis tradition, the human who has become divine.

On the other hand, in the earlier chapters of the Similitudes, the Son of Man does get to sit on that throne; here we have the notion of the theophany, the divine figure who will reveal himself in the man. In these chapters, the Son of Man, who also carries, as we have seen, the title of Messiah, has the role of eschatological judge (judge at the final assizes). This clearly comes out from a way of reading Daniel 7:14—"To him was given dominion and kingdom. All peoples, nations, and languages will serve him. His dominion is an everlasting dominion, which will not pass away, and his kingdom is indestructible"—in which the assignment of sovereignty to the Son of Man is primarily constituted via his role as this judge at the last time.[16] In these chapters, the Son of Man is made, like Moses, to sit on the divine throne itself (62:2, 5; 69:27, 29; 61:8). Following the principle just articulated—that one who sits on the divine throne either alongside or sometimes in place of God is himself divine and a sharer in God's divinity—then the Son of Man certainly fits this description in the Similitudes. He is, moreover, clearly the object of worship in this text also (46:5; 48:5; 62:6, 9). But he is not yet Enoch. Enoch in these chapters is the seer, not the seen.

We can observe, then, two parallel Enoch traditions, growing out of 1 Enoch 14 and Daniel 7: a tradition of an exalted divinized human, on one hand, and on the other, a tradition of a second God-like Redeemer who comes down to save Israel. What we don't have yet is the identification or merging of that divinized human with the anthropized divinity, such as we find in the Gospel of Mark and its followers.

Where this comes together is in chapters 70–71 of the Similitudes, which must be seen as an independent strand of very ancient tradition, in which the two originally separate ideas of God becoming man and a man becoming God are fused.[17] In the first part of the work, the Son of Man is explicitly described as preexistent to creation, while Enoch is the seventh born human after Adam. Enoch, the seventh of the patriarchs from Adam, bears strong connections with the seventh of the antediluvian Babylonian kings, Enmeduranki, who was of human descent but was taken up into heaven. Among the features that Enoch shares with his Babylonian ancestor is being seated on a throne in heaven in the presence of the gods and taught wisdom there.[18] This makes clear why an identification could be made. As in the Book of Daniel itself, different texts have been quilted together to make a single theological statement.

The whole story of Enoch as the Son of Man all begins with the verses about Enoch in the Book of Genesis. The story of Enoch as we have it in those few enigmatic verses of Genesis 5 reads:

> [21]*And Enoch lived sixty and five years, and begat*
> *Methuselah:*
> [22]*And Enoch walked with God after he begat*

> *Methuselah three hundred years, and begat sons*
> *and daughters:*
> [23]*And all the days of Enoch were three hundred sixty*
> *and five years:*
> [24]*And Enoch walked with God: and he was not; for*
> *God took him.*

This terminology is unique in the Bible; of no one else is it said that "he was not." It cannot be interpreted, therefore, to mean simply that he died. Something special happened to Enoch: not only was he shown visions and wonders and given understanding, but he was with God and he was not; he was taken by God. Chapters 70–71 likely were added to the Enoch text from some other version to answer this very question, precisely because they fill out the story of Enoch's apotheosis. They explain what happens when Enoch walks with God; he becomes the Son of Man, and that is why he was no longer among humans. This literary move, interpreting the obscure text of Genesis by splicing together two apparently originally separate texts about Enoch, has had an enormous theological effect.

This movement of the theology is indicated precisely at the difficult textual moment in which "that angel came to me and greeted me with his voice and said to me, 'You are that son of man who was born for righteousness, and righteousness dwells on you, and the righteousness of the

Head of Days will not forsake you.' " Two traditions are combined in the Similitudes of Enoch: the preexistent, second God, Redeemer of Daniel, now not only described as the Son of Man but so named, and the exalted seventh antediluvian sage, Enoch, who went up to heaven because he walked with God, and God took him, and he was not. Once this stitch in time has been made, we must read the text as implying that Enoch was from the beginning the Messiah, the Son of Man, hidden from the beginning, then sent to earth in human form, and now exalted once again to his former state.

This theological innovation must have taken place before the actual writing of the Similitudes of Enoch in the first century A.D.; it is of major importance for understanding the similar development that we can observe in the Christology of the New Testament. Just as the Son of Man in the Similitudes is a preexistent divine figure holding the dignity of the second divine throne and afforded all the privileges and sovereignty of the one like a son of man in Daniel, so too the preexistent Son of Man who lies behind the Gospels. This divine figure became ultimately identified with Enoch in two ways, one via his becoming Enoch when Enoch is exalted into heaven and one in his being revealed as having been Enoch all along. This is the paradox that inhabits the Gospel story of the Christ as well: on one hand, the Son of Man is a divine person, part of God, coexistent with God for all eternity, revealed on earth in the human Jesus; on the other hand, the human Jesus has been exalted and raised to divine status. To use once more the terms afforded us by Moshe Idel, we have here an instance of the "Son of Man" as apotheosis, a man becoming God, and at the same time, the "Son of Man" as theophany, the self-revelation of God in a human.[19] To be sure, the emphasis in the Enochian version is on the apotheosis, in the Gospel on the theophany, and that will be an important part of the further story, but I think it well established that both elements are present in both versions of the *Jewish* Son of Man tradition. Further examination of the history of the Enoch tradition will help prepare us to understand this better.

Enoch and the Christ Son of Man

The second book of 1 Enoch, the Similitudes of Enoch, is a product roughly of the same time as the Gospel of Mark—but there is a still earlier first book. Known as the Book of the Watchers, this first book of 1 Enoch is probably as old as the third century B.C. Enoch 14, from the Book of the Watchers, is thematically directly related to Daniel 7, and very probably its progenitor, which is to say that the vision of Daniel was based on an even older literary apocalyptic tradition.[20] In 1 Enoch 1 14–16, we find the following elements in order: Enoch has dreams and visions; "In a vision, I saw" (14:2); clouds summoned him and winds carried him up; he sees a throne with wheels like the shining sun; streams of fire go out from under the throne; God's raiment is whiter than snow; Enoch is called to God's presence who hears his voice saying: "Fear not, Enoch, go, say the message."[21] Now there may be no doubt that this text draws on the prophetic commissioning of Ezekiel in the prophet's book, chapters 1–2, incorporating as well Ezekiel's tour of the heavenly temple in chapters 40–44. It is perhaps only somewhat less apparent that the author of Daniel 7, in turn, is drawing on this chapter in 1 Enoch and developing it further in accord with his own theological traditions and other apocalyptic sources that include the vision of the second throne and the second divine person.

Whatever the precise case on the genetic relationship, it is clear that the author of the Similitudes, who clearly derives his Son of Man figure from Daniel 7, could easily have identified the one like a son of man from Daniel with Enoch as described in Enoch 14. Both arrive with clouds; both are brought near the Ancient of Days by one of the angels; both include the description of the throne as having before it streams of blazing fire and of his person as wearing garments brighter than snow. The two texts are thus almost certainly related, with the most likely scenario invoking dependence of Daniel on the most ancient part of 1 Enoch, the Book of the Watchers.[22]

The author of the Similitudes associated the Enoch of Enoch 14 and the one like a son of man of Daniel 7 and concluded, quite naturally, in Enoch 71 that "you [Enoch] are the Son of Man." A crucial step in the developed messianic idea thus had been taken: the merger of the second God, heavenly Redeemer figure and an earthly savior exalted into heaven.[23] We can detect in the Similitudes of Enoch the actual tracks of a religious history in which two originally independent strands of tradition have been combined into one. On one hand, we see the development of the one like a son of man of Daniel 7 from a simile into a title; we can literally see this development taking place on the page.[24] On the other hand, we see the tradition of the seventh antediluvian human king who was exalted and given a place in heaven, which is one of the most powerful themes of the whole Enoch work. In chapter 71 of the Similitudes we observe these two traditions being combined into one and the two figures of Enoch and the Son of Man coming together. The complex, doubled story of the Son of Man had already been prepared for in pre-Jesus Jewish speculation and was extant at the time of his life: it already included the two elements of a Son of Man who was the preexistent, transcendent Messiah and the element of the human being who would be the embodiment of that Messiah on earth and be exalted and merged with him. Thus was born the Christ, not quite a historical virgin birth or creation out of nothing but the fulfillment of the highest and most powerful aspirations of the Jewish people.

The Wisdom elements of the newly born Messiah figure come in, I think, together with Enoch, carrying in their wake the early readings of Proverbs 8 and the Logos traditions as well.[25] The Son of Man of the Similitudes judges and condemns, was created before the universe like (or even as) the Wisdom of Proverbs, is equated with the Messiah (but not the human messiah), is assimilated to the Deity, and is portrayed as a proper recipient of worship. All that was required then for the full picture was the association of Enoch, the human exalted to heaven, with the Son of Man and the full Christological transformation will have taken place.

All of the elements of Christology are essentially in place then in the Similitudes. We have a preexistent heavenly figure (identified as well with Wisdom), who is the Son of Man. We have an earthly life, a human sage exalted into heaven at the end of an earthly career, enthroned in heaven at the right side of the Ancient of Days as the preexistent and forever reigning Son of Man. While the Gospels are certainly not drawing on the Similitudes, the Similitudes help illuminate the cultural, religious context in which the Gospels were produced. As New Testament scholar Richard Baukham so well phrased it, "It can readily be seen that early Christians applied to Jesus all the well-established and well-organized characteristics of the unique divine identity in order, quite clearly and precisely, to include Jesus in the unique identity of the one God of Israel."[26] In the worship of the Messiah/Son of Man/Enoch in the Similitudes of Enoch, we find the closest parallel to the Gospels. Since there is no reason in the world to think that either of these texts influenced the other, together they provide strong evidence for the confluence of ideas about the human Messiah, the son of David, and the divine Messiah, the Son of Man, in Judaism by at least the first century A.D. and probably earlier.[27]

Fourth Ezra and the Son of Man

The Similitudes of Enoch was not by any means the only first-century Jewish text other than the Gospels in which the Son of Man was identified as the Messiah. In another text from the same time as the Similitudes and the Gospel of Mark, the apocalypse known as Fourth Ezra, we also find a divine figure based on Daniel 7 and identified with the Messiah. Fascinatingly enough, we also find evidence in this text for yet another attempt to suppress this religious idea, thus adding to our evidence that the idea was controversial among Jews entirely outside of the question of Jesus' divinity and Messiahship. This text is, as we shall see, dependent as well on Daniel 7 and provides us with one more option for an interpretation of the Son of Man figure that is important for understanding the Gospels. In chapter 13 of that text, we meet the Danielic one like a son of man once again. In some ways the Son of Man figure in Fourth Ezra is even closer to the one of the Gospels than the version in Enoch:

After seven days I dreamed a dream in the night; [2]and behold a great wind arose from the sea so that it stirred up all its waves. [3]And I looked, and behold, this wind made something like the figure of a man come out of the heat of the sea. And I looked, and behold, that man flew with the clouds of heaven; and wherever he turned his face to look, everything under his gaze trembled, [4]and wherever the voice of his mouth issued forth, all who heard his voice melted as wax melts when it feels the fire.

[5]After this I looked, and behold, an innumerable multitude of men were gathered together from the four winds of heaven to make war against the man who came up out of the sea. [6]And I looked, and behold, he carved out for himself a great mountain, and flew upon it. [7]And I tried to see the region or place from which the mountain was carved, but I could not.

[8]After this I looked, and behold, all who had gathered together against him, to wage war with him, were much afraid, yet dared to fight. [9]And when he saw the onrush of the approaching multitude,

he neither lifted his hand nor held a sword or any weapon of war; [10]but saw only how he sent forth from his mouth as it were a stream of fire, and from his lips a flaming breath, and from his tongue he shot forth a storm of fiery coals.[28]

Needless to say, the enemies of the man are then burnt to a crisp, if not worse than that. This passage, of course, is clearly based on a reading of Daniel 7, as are the Enoch passages discussed above. Even more sharply (partly owing to its relative density) than in Enoch, the Ezra passage makes absolutely clear the combination of the divine Son of Man and the Redeemer or Messiah—a high Christology indeed, and, of course, one that is independent of the Jesus movement entirely.* Closely paralleling the Enoch passage as well, here too close reference is made to Daniel by citing the appearance of the figure as a man and only then referring to him as *the* Man. Once again, we see a simile become a Redeemer. And since the simile clearly refers to a divine figure (a divine warrior), the Redeemer is held to be divine.[29] As Stone remarks, "It is quite interesting that the passages referring to breath or word are

---

* This point is perhaps most sharply brought out in Fourth Ezra 12:32, in which it is insisted that the heavenly Son of Man comes from the posterity of David, "even though it is not apparent why a descendant of David should come on the clouds." A.Y. Collins and J.J. Collins, *King and Messiah as Son of God: Divine, Human, and Angelic Messianic Figures in Biblical and Related Literature* (Grand Rapids, MI: W.B. Eerdmans, 2008), 207.

applied both to God and to the redeemer, but, other than our present passage, the passages in which fire is specifically mentioned all refer to God. Therefore, the present passage is unique in this respect and serves to emphasize the cosmic role of the human figure, which in any case many other elements of the text highlight."[30] Pushing the point just a bit further, we arrive at the same sort of argument that has been advanced for the one like a son of man of Daniel, namely, that if it is only YHVH who comes riding on clouds, then here too that figure is a divine one. Ezra's Man is divine as well.

The vision concludes:

> [12]After this I saw the same man come down from the mountain and call to him another multitude which was peaceable. [13]Then the forms of many people came to him, some of whom were joyful and some sorrowful; some of them were bound and some were bringing others as offerings.

This bit of the text nails down the claim that the Man, the Messiah, is God, for this eschatological vision with its offerings is drawn directly from Isaiah 66:20: "And they shall bring all your brethren from all the nations as an offering to the Lord." Those others brought here as offerings then are brought to the Lord, the *kurios*, the Son of Man, the Redeemer. Note that the same sort of argument that is used to prove the divinity of Jesus—namely, the application of verses to him that are in the Bible predicated of YHVH—works here as well for the Man. This Man is the Lord. If Jesus is God, then, by the very same reasoning, so is this Man.

Here too, as in Daniel 7 itself, we find another witness to a pre-Christian religious conflict within Israel between those who accepted the very ancient idea of an older-appearing divine figure and a younger one who shares his throne and to whom the older one gives authority and other Jews who rejected this idea as a seeming contradiction of monotheism.* Two different strands of the religious imagination, one in which the ancient binitarianness of Israel's God is essentially preserved and transformed and one in which that duality has been more thoroughly

---

* This point is supported by a very important observation made by Michael Stone: the description of the Redeemer in chapter 13 that is being presented here is unique within Fourth Ezra itself. In all other moments within that text, the Redeemer, while in some sense preexistent, seems to fall much more toward the pole of the human Davidic Messiah tradition than the second divinity that we find in Daniel 7, the Similitudes of Enoch, and Fourth Ezra 13. Moreover, as also observed sharply by Stone, the interpretation of the vision in the second half of chapter 13 suppresses the cosmic divine aspect of the Man. What has not been noticed, I think, is that this matches up beautifully with Daniel 7 itself, in which the vision of a second divine figure, the one like a son of man, is also rendered as entirely human and as an allegorical symbol by the interpretation in the second half of the chapter. Michael Edward Stone, *Fourth Ezra: A Commentary on the Book 1 Fourth Ezra,* ed. Frank Moore Cross (Minneapolis: Fortress Press, 1990), 211–13.

suppressed, live side by side in the Jewish thought world of the Second Temple and beyond, being mixed in different ways but also contesting each other and sometimes seeking to oust the other completely. This background, I think, explains much of the religion of the Gospels as a continuation and development of a strand of Israelite religion that is very ancient indeed.

The usage of "Son of Man" in the Gospels joins up with the evidence of such usage from Similitudes to lead us to consider this term used in this way (and, more important, its implication of a second divinity incorporated as the Messiah implied by it) as the common coin—which again I emphasize does not mean universal or uncontested—of Judaism already before Jesus.[31]

The Gospel of Mark and the Similitudes of Enoch are independent witnesses to a Jewish pattern of religion at their shared time. Texts are not religions (any more than a map is territory), but they are evidence of the religion, tips of icebergs that suggest massive religious developments and formations below the surface, or, perhaps better put, aboveground nodes on a rhizomic system underground that suggest the shape of the rhizomes. The territory was surely as bumpy and variegated as an earthly territory would be; as Carsten Colpe has put it, "The differences in the functions of the Son of Man may be explained by the differences between the groups which expected Him and the times in which they did so."[32]

The great innovation of the Gospels is only this: to declare that the Son of Man is here already, that he walks among us. As opposed to Enoch, who will be in those last days the Messiah Son of Man, Jesus already is. As opposed to the Son of Man flying on the clouds, who is a vision for the future, Jesus has come, declare the Gospels and the believers. The last days are right now, proclaims the Gospel. All of the ideas about Christ are old; the new is Jesus. There is nothing in the doctrine of the Christ that is new save the declaration of *this* man as the Son of Man. This is, of course, an enormous declaration, a huge innovation in itself and one that has had fateful historical consequences.

3

Jesus Kept Kosher

MOST (IF NOT ALL) OF the ideas and practices of the Jesus
movement of the first century and the beginning of the
second century—and even later—can be safely understood as part of the ideas and practices that we understand
to be the Judaism of this period. The ideas of Trinity and
incarnation, or certainly the germs of those ideas, were
already present among Jewish believers well before Jesus
came on the scene to incarnate in himself, as it were, those
theological notions and take up his messianic calling.

However, the Jewish background of the ideas of the
Jesus movement is only one piece of the new picture I'm
sketching here. Much of the most compelling evidence
for the Jewishness of the early Jesus communities comes
from the Gospels themselves. The Gospels, of course,
are almost always understood as the marker of a very
great break from Judaism. Over and over, we find within

interpretations of them (whether pious or scholarly) statements of what a radical break is constituted by Jesus' teaching with respect to the "Judaism" of his day. The notions of Judaism as legalistic and rule-bound, as a grim realm of religious anxiety versus Jesus' completely new teaching of love and faith, die very hard.

Even among those who recognize that Jesus himself may very well have been a pious Jew—a special teacher, to be sure, but not one instituting a consequential break with Judaism—the Gospels, and especially Mark, are taken as the sign of the rupture of Christianity, of its near-total overturn, of the forms of traditional piety. One of the most radical of these displacements is, according to nearly all views, the total rejection by Mark's Jesus of Jewish dietary practices, the kosher rules.

Counter to most views of the matter, according to the Gospel of Mark, Jesus kept kosher, which is to say that he saw himself not as abrogating the Torah but as defending it. There was controversy with some other Jewish leaders as to how best to observe the Law, but none, I will argue, about *whether* to observe it. According to Mark (and Matthew even more so), far from abandoning the laws and practices of the Torah, Jesus was a staunch defender of the Torah against what he perceived to be threats to it from the Pharisees.

The Pharisees were a kind of reform movement within the Jewish people that was centered on Jerusalem and

Judaea. The Pharisees sought to convert other Jews to their way of thinking about God and the Torah, a way of thinking that incorporated seeming changes in the written Torah's practices that were mandated by what the Pharisees called "the tradition of the Elders." The justification of these reforms in the name of an oral Torah, a tradition passed down by the Elders from Sinai on, would have been experienced by many traditional Jews as a radical change, especially when it involved changing the traditional ways that they and their ancestors had kept the Torah for generations immemorial. At least some of these pharisaic innovations may very well have represented changes in religious practice that took place during the Babylonian Exile, while the Jews who remained "in the land" continued their ancient practices. It is quite plausible, therefore, that other Jews, such as the Galilean Jesus, would reject angrily such ideas as an affront to the Torah and as sacrilege.

Jesus' Judaism was a conservative reaction against some radical innovations in the Law stemming from the Pharisees and Scribes of Jerusalem.

The Gospel of Mark provides the bedrock for this new understanding of Jesus, one with consequences not only for how we understand that Gospel but also for our reading of the Gospels more generally. In the twentieth century a new historical notion of the relations of the Gospels to one another began to form and is now held in most (but not all) scholarly quarters. Mark is now considered the earliest of the Gospels by most scholars today, who date it to some time right after the destruction of the Temple in A.D. 70. Matthew and Luke are taken to have used Mark and modified him for their purposes as well as adding other sources for the Gospel, notably a source that communicated many sayings of Jesus.

This new and compelling explanation of how the Synoptic Gospels relate to each other has the perhaps unintended consequence of making the idea of Jesus' near-total abrogation of the Law the very founding moment of the Christian movement. If, as most scholars have opined, the author of Mark was a Gentile and one rather ignorant of Jewish ways at that, then the very beginnings of the Jesus movement are already implicated in a rejection of the Jewish way of life. On the other hand, if Mark was himself a member of a Jewish community and so was his Jesus, then the beginnings of Christianity can be considered in a very different light, as a version, perhaps a radical one, of the religion of the Jews. Jesus, in this view, was fighting not against Judaism but within it—an entirely different matter. Far from being a marginal Jew, Jesus was a leader of one type of Judaism that was being marginalized by another group, the Pharisees, and he was fighting against them as dangerous innovators. This view of Christianity as but a variation within Judaism, and even a highly conservative and traditionalist one, goes to the heart of our description of the relations in the second, third, and fourth centuries between so-called Jewish Christianity and its early rival, the so-called Gentile Christianity that was eventually (after some centuries) to win the day.

Mark 7 and the Non-Parting of the Ways

In conventional readings of the Gospel of Mark, Jesus' relationship to the Jewish dietary laws is taken as a watershed moment in religious history, when one set of fundamental beliefs is cast out in favor of a new worldview. For centuries, Christian preachers, scholars, and lay readers of Mark have read the Gospel as teaching us not only that Jesus did not keep kosher but also that he permitted all foods that the Torah had forbidden Jews to eat.[1] This would be a shift of no small moment, as indeed the dietary laws were then and remain today one of the very hallmarks of Jewish religious practice. If Mark has been misread, however, and his Jesus did not abandon or abrogate such basic Jewish practices as keeping kosher, then our entire sense of where the Jesus movement stands in relation to the Judaism of its time is quite changed. In short, if the earliest of Christians believed that Jesus kept kosher, then we have good reason to view that Christianity as another contending branch of Judaism.

The question of the "Jewishness" of Mark lies at the very heart of our understanding of the historical meaning of the Jesus movement in its earliest period. Jesus was, according to the view I defend here, not fighting against the Jews or Judaism but with some Jews for what he considered to be the right kind of Judaism. As we have seen in the past two chapters, this kind of Judaism included the idea of a second divine person who would be found on earth in human form as the Messiah (and in the person of that Jesus). The only controversy surrounding Jesus was whether this son of the carpenter of Nazareth truly was the one for whom the Jews were waiting. Taking himself to be that very Jewish Messiah, Son of Man, however, Jesus surely would not have spoken contemptuously of the Torah but would have upheld it.

As read by most commentators, Mark 7 establishes the beginning of the so-called parting of the ways between Judaism and Christianity. This is because, according to the traditional interpretation and virtually all modern scholarly ones, in this chapter Jesus declares a major aspect of the Torah's laws, the laws of kashrut (keeping kosher), no longer valid, thus representing a major rupture with the beliefs and practices of virtually all other Jews, pharisaic or not. The representatives of what are arguably the three most central and important scholarly biblical commentary series in the United States, ranging from the Word series for evangelical scholars to the Anchor Bible for the non-confessional and more general (but advanced) audience and then to the very scholarly and secular Hermeneia—which, taken together, represent the closest thing we have to an authoritative modern reading of the passage—all agree on this in their commentaries on Mark 7, even while disagreeing on much else. Thus Adela Yarbro Collins, in her Hermeneia commentary, writes of verse 19 ("and thus he purified all foods"), "The comment of v. 19c [third clause of v. 19] takes a giant step further and implies, at the very least, that the observance of the food laws for followers of Jesus is not obligatory."[2] In the evangelical scholarly Word commentary, Robert A. Guelich too writes, "Jesus' saying in 7:15 explained with reference to what one eats by 7:18b–19 means that no foods, even those forbidden by the Levitical law (Lev 11–15), could defile a person before God. In essence, Jesus 'makes all foods clean.' "[3] In his commentary in the time-honored Anchor Bible, Joel Marcus writes that "anyone who did what the Markan Jesus does in our passage, denying this dietary distinction and declaring all food to be permissible (7:19), would immediately be identified as a seducer who led the people's heart astray from God (cf. 7:6) and from the holy commandment he had given to Moses (cf. 7:8, 9, 13)."[4] This view is the commonly held interpretation of the passage in both the pious and scholarly traditions.[5]

But did the Markan Jesus do this sacrilegious thing, and is this passage truly a parting of the ways between Judaism and Christianity? Reading the text backward from later Christian practices and beliefs about the written Torah and its abrogations, interpreters and scholars have found a point of origin, even a legend of origin, for their version of Christianity in this chapter. In contrast, reading the text through lenses colored by years of immersion in the Jewish religious literature of the times around Jesus and the evangelists produces a very different perspective on the chapter from the one that has come to be so dominant. Anchoring Mark in its proper historical and cultural context, we find a very different text indeed, one that reveals an inner Jewish controversy, rather than an abrogation of the Torah and denial of Judaism.

It will be well to have the entire narrative in mind for this discussion, so let me begin by citing the text from the NRSV translation:

Now when the Pharisees and some of the scribes who had come from Jerusalem gathered around him, [2]they noticed that some of his disciples were eating with defiled hands, that is, without washing them. [3](For the Pharisees, and all the Jews, do not eat unless they thoroughly[6] wash their hands, thus observing the tradition of the elders; [4]and they do not eat anything from the market unless they wash it; and there are also many other traditions that they observe, the washing of cups, pots, and bronze kettles.) [5]So the Pharisees and the scribes asked him,

"Why do your disciples not live according to the tradition of the elders, but eat with defiled hands?" [6]He said to them, "Isaiah prophesied rightly about you hypocrites, as it is written, 'This people honors me with their lips, but their hearts are far from me; [7]in vain do they worship me, teaching human precepts as doctrines.' [8]You abandon the commandment of God and hold to human tradition." [9]Then he said to them, "You have a fine way of rejecting the commandment of God in order to keep your tradition! [10]For Moses said, 'Honor your father and your mother'; and, 'Whoever curses of father or mother must surely die.'[7] [11]But you say that if anyone tells father or mother, 'Whatever support you might have had from me is Corban' (that is, an offering to God)— [12]then you no longer permit doing anything for a father or mother, [13]thus making void the word of God through your tradition that you have handed on. And you do many things like this." [14]Then he called the crowd again and said to them, "Listen to me, all of you, and understand: [15]there is nothing outside a person that by going in can defile, but the things that come out are what defile." [16, 17]When he had left the crowd and entered the house, his disciples asked him about the parable. [18]He said to them, "Then do you also fail to understand? Do you not see that whatever goes into a person from outside cannot defile, [19]since it enters, not the heart but the stomach, and goes out into the sewer?" (Thus he declared all foods clean.) [20]And he said, "It is what comes out of a person that defiles. [21]For it is from within, from the human heart, that evil intentions come: fornication, theft, murder, [22]adultery, avarice, wickedness, deceit, licentiousness, envy, slander, pride, folly. [23]All these evil things come from within, and they defile a person."

There is such a long history of interpreting this passage that it alone would fill a book. The demons that beset the "tradition history" of this passage are legion; some scholars consider some verses original and others later additions, while others argue just the opposite as to which verses were original and which added later. I am going to cast the demons out by ignoring them and trying to read the text as it is. My goal is to get closer to a sense of what the canonical Gospel of Mark might have meant in its original cultural, religious context, a context that has to be thoroughly known and clearly articulated to do its interpretative work.

The first thing that must be acknowledged is that while the *readers* of Mark are clearly expected to be far away from traditional Jewish practice as well as from the Aramaic and Hebrew languages, the *writer* of Mark is anything but distant from and ignorant of these matters. He demonstrates, in fact, a fine and clear understanding of

Jewish practice and the Jewish languages, as does his Jesus. This distinction has been missed in much of the earlier work on Mark and especially on this chapter.

In contrast to virtually all Christian commentators, I propose that whatever Jesus is portrayed as doing in the above text from Mark—including "and thus he purified all foods"—it is not permitting the eating of all foods, even if we accept every word of the passage as it is before us in the text.

In order to make this proposition stick, it's very important that we make some distinctions between different domains of the Torah's law and especially the dietary laws, for there has been much confusion on this score. To call food kosher refers to its permissibility or impermissibility for eating by Jews as defined in the Bible and the later rabbinic literature. Among the foods forbidden are non-ruminants such as pigs and rabbits, birds of prey, and sea creatures that have no fins or scales. Meat, to be kosher, has also to be slaughtered in a special way deemed painless to the animal, and milk and meat foods must be kept separate from each other. These laws are observed to the letter by pious Jews even today. Although, somewhat confusingly, animals that are not kosher are referred to as "impure" animals, these kashrut (kosher) laws have nothing to do with purity and impurity of the body or other items. There is a separate set of rules that define when any food—kosher or not—is pure or impure, depending on how that food was handled and what other things it may have come into contact with. Indeed, there are kosher foods that in *some* circumstances and for *some* Jews were forbidden to be eaten, despite the fact that they are in themselves made of entirely kosher ingredients, cooked in kosher pots, and not incorporating milk with meat. Such foods have become impure through some mishap, such as being touched by a person with a flux from his or her body. While all Jews are forbidden always to eat pork, lobster, milk and meat together, and meat that has not been properly slaughtered, only some Jews, some of the time, are forbidden to eat kosher food that has become contaminated with ritual impurity. While in English they are sometimes confused, the system of purity and impurity laws and the system of dietary laws are two different systems within the Torah's rules for eating, and Mark and Jesus knew the difference. One of the biggest obstacles to this understanding has been in the use of the English words "clean" and "unclean" to refer both to the laws of permitted and forbidden foods and to the laws of pollution or impurity and purity. These translate two entirely different sets of Hebrew words, *muttar* and *tahor*. It would be better to translate the first set by "permitted" and "forbidden" and use "clean" and "unclean," or "pure" and "impure," only for the latter set.

On one hand, the Torah lists various species of birds, fish and other sea creatures, and land animals that may never be eaten. It also forbids the eating of the sciatic nerve, the consumption of certain kinds of fat on otherwise kosher animals, the consumption of blood, and cooking a kid in its mother's milk (taken early on by most Jews, apparently, to mean not to cook meat and milk together). Together these rules make up what is called the Jewish dietary laws or kosher rules. As I have mentioned, they apply to all Jews everywhere and always.

Purity and impurity, or pollution (*tuma'h vetaharah*), is an entirely separate system of rules and regulations that apply to a different sphere of life, namely, the laws having to do with the touching of various objects, such as dead humans or humans who have touched dead humans and not washed properly, as well as with other causes of impurity such as skin diseases or fluxes from the body, including menstrual blood and semen (but not excreta), which render a person "impure" according to the Torah but carry no moral opprobrium. People may become impure without any deed on their parts at all. In fact, most Israelites were impure most of the time (and today we all are all the time), since it requires a trip to the Temple to be purified from some kinds of ubiquitous impurities. The touch of such "impure" persons renders certain perfectly kosher foods forbidden to be eaten by Priests or by Israelites who are entering the Temple. During Second Temple times, there is much evidence that many Jews sought to avoid such impurity and to purify themselves as quickly as they could according to the rules from the Torah even if they were not planning to go to the Temple. The Pharisees extended these practices, even legislating that eating kosher food that has been in contact with impurities renders one impure.

According to the biblical system (to which, apparently, the Galilean practice might very well have corresponded), the two sets of rules are kept quite strictly apart. A Jew did not eat non-kosher food, but rules around defiled kosher food depended on various circumstances of the eater's life and certainly did not render the body of the eater impure. The pharisaic tradition seems to have extended that prohibition against eating defiled kosher food and also rendered the eater him- or herself impure through this eating. The Pharisees sought to convince other Jews to adhere to their new standards of strictness (this is apparently the meaning of them going over land and sea to convert—they were attempting to "convert" other Jews, not Gentiles).[8] They therefore instituted a practice of ritual hand purification by pouring water over the hands before eating bread, so that the hands would not make the bread impure.

Thus, in order to understand what Jesus is talking about in the Gospel, we must have a clearer sense of what his terminology might have meant in his cultural world, not ours.[9] In the Gospel, we are told that Pharisees have come from Jerusalem, apparently to proselytize for their understanding of the Torah and its rules, including these extensions of the purity regulations, such as the washing of the hands. Jesus protests, asserting that foods that go into the body don't make the body impure; only things that come out of the body have that power to contaminate. So really what the Gospel describes is a Jesus who rejects the pharisaic extension of these purity laws beyond their original specific biblical foundations. He is not rejecting the Torah's rules and practices but upholding them.

In contrast to many earlier views, it's clear that Mark knew very well what he was talking about when he discussed the pharisaic ritual practices and purity rules. The clearest demonstration of this involves a word in the Greek that is usually obscured in English translations of Mark 7:3: "οἱ γὰρ Φαρισαῖοι καὶ πάντες οἱ Ἰουδαῖοι ἐὰν μὴ πυγμῇ νίψωνται τὰς χεῖρας οὐκ ἐσθίουσιν, κρατοῦντες τὴν παράδοσιν τῶν πρεσβυτέρων [For the Pharisees and all of the Judaeans do not eat unless they wash the hands *with a fist*,[10] according to the tradition of the Elders]." Scholarship has only recently adopted the translation "with a fist" after centuries of emendation of the text against the dominant textual tradition.[11] The usage "with a fist," albeit for fighting or hitting, is attested in the ancient Greek translation of the Bible, the Septuagint, more than once (Exodus 21:8; Isaiah 58:4). As anyone who has seen Jews actually performing the ritual of hand washing would guess immediately, Mark is referring to the process of forming a loose fist with one hand and pouring water over that fist with the other.[12] I would suggest, moreover, that Mark's emphasis on "with a fist" might well be a description of the practice itself but also an allusive, almost punning reference to the pugnaciousness of these Pharisees.[13] But regardless of that last point, when the Gospel is understood in this manner it provides incredibly precious evidence, available nowhere else, of the great antiquity of a Jewish practice otherwise attested only later. If Mark was such a close observer and manifests such intimate knowledge of pharisaic practice, then my assumption as I read the passage is that he knew of what he spoke all the way down. This suggests strongly that his perspective (as well as that of his Jesus) is firmly from within the Jewish world—nearly the opposite of what has been usually said of Mark.

Yair Furstenberg, a young Talmud scholar at the Hebrew University, has recently provided a convincing explanation of the basic controversy between Jesus and those Pharisees. Furstenberg writes that Jesus' statement needs to be read literally to mean that the body is made impure not through ingesting impure foods but only through various substances that come out from the body. As noted, according to the Torah it is not what goes into the body that makes one impure but only things that come out of the body: fluxes of blood, semen, and gonorrhea. The only food, according to the Torah, that renders a body impure is carrion—certainly not the eating of permitted food that has become impure, or of forbidden foods generally. According to the Talmud itself, it was the Rabbis (or the legendary Pharisees) who innovated the washing of the hands before meals—which implies that the ingesting of defiled or polluted foods renders one impure. It was thus against those pharisaic innovations, which they are trying to foist on his disciples, that Jesus railed, and not against the keeping of kosher at all.[14] This is a debate between Jews about the correct way to keep the Torah, not an attack on the Torah. Furstenberg has brilliantly argued that in its original sense, Jesus' attack on the Pharisees here is literal: they *have* changed the rules of the Torah. This is made clear in a key rabbinic text, which, while much later than the Gospel, ascribes a change in the halakha to the time of Mark:

> These categories render the priestly offering unfit [to be eaten by the Priests]: He who eats directly impure food; . . . and he who drinks impure fluids; . . . and the hands. (Zabim 5:12)

If someone eats or drinks impure food, then his touch renders the priestly portion impure and unfit for the priests.[15] This innovative ruling is, moreover, explicitly connected in the list with the hands as well, just as the Markan Jesus associates them. Now, these rulings are explicitly marked within the talmudic tradition as being of rabbinic origin and not as rulings of the Torah. That is to say, the classical Rabbis themselves maintained a distinction between what was written in the Torah and what had been added by them or by their pharisaic forebears. They explicitly remark that here we have a pharisaic extension of the Torah, thus confirming what Jesus said. According to the Torah, only that which comes out of the body (fluxes of various types) can contaminate, not foods that go in.[16] Thus, if the Pharisees argue that food itself contaminates, that is a change in the law.

The attack on hand washing in the story is, moreover, consistent with Jesus' subsequent attack on the vow that releases one from supporting ones' parents:

> [11]But you say that if anyone tells father or mother, "Whatever support you might have had from me is Corban" (that is, an offering to God) [12]then you no longer permit doing anything for a father or mother, [13]thus making void the word of God through your tradition that you have handed on. And you do many things like this.

Jesus here accuses the Pharisees of having abandoned the plain sense of the Torah, which requires that Jews support their elderly parents. They have allegedly done this sacrilege by asserting that one who takes a vow not to allow his parents to have use of anything he has as if it were a sacrifice dedicated to God has effectively prohibited himself from providing such support.* This represents another instance in which the Pharisees apparently supplant the Torah with their "tradition of the Elders." Once again, Jesus and Mark have got it exactly right in terms of the Torah and the oral traditions exemplified by the Pharisees and other innovators. For Jesus (Mark) the "tradition of the elders" is a *human* creation, as opposed to the written Torah, which is divine. Hence the force of the citation from Isaiah, in which Jesus says to them, "Isaiah prophesied rightly about you hypocrites, as it is written, 'This people honors me with their lips, but their hearts are far from me; ⁷in vain do they worship me, teaching human precepts as doctrines.' ⁸You abandon the commandment of God and hold to human tradition."

From Jesus' point of view, the "tradition of the elders"—later called the oral Torah—is exactly "human precepts" being taught as doctrines, as in the prophetic formulation. For the Pharisees, and later for the Rabbis, the "tradition of the elders" is divine word and not human precepts (though they were transmitted orally rather than

---

* The later Rabbis, at least from the second century on, developed a method for invalidating such a vow, which indeed goes against the Torah. It is hard to assess the historical validity of the Markan Jesus' claim against the Pharisees, but it cannot be denied that it might very well have been the case, especially given his accuracy in other matters of Jewish, and especially pharisaic, practices.

scripturally).[17] In this case, moreover, we have an admittedly pharisaic innovation, contested even by some other Pharisees. No wonder that Jesus would balk and protest. What I hope to have shown till now in this section is that when Mark wrote the words καθαρίζων πάντα τὰ βρώματα "purifying all foods," there is little reason to believe that it meant "thus he permitted all foods," but rather, "thus he purified all foods," meaning that he rejected the extra-stringent laws of defiled foods to which the Pharisees were so devoted—not the kosher rules.[18] Jesus was certainly not sanctioning here the eating of bacon and eggs; rather, exactly as the text says, he was permitting the eating of bread without ritual washing of the hands, quite a different matter. The controversy ends where it began, in a contest over the question of bodily impurity caused by the ingestion of impure foods. It is highly unlikely that in its original context Mark was read as meaning that Jesus had abrogated the rules of forbidden and permitted animals.

What makes this not merely "a halakhic [legalistic] squabble between first-century Jews" (to echo a colorful bon mot of John Paul Meier's) is Jesus' use of the controversy to make a strong theological claim in the form of the parable. Whether or not the Pharisees were hypocrites (I would imagine that some were and some were not), it is certainly the case that to concern oneself with extraordinary performances of external piety while ignoring (or worse) the ethical and spiritual requirements of the Torah is poor religion, on the order perhaps of preaching that Jesus is love but hates homosexuals. We should remember, however, that "in general, in ancient Jewish and Christian contexts a 'hypocrite' is a person whose interpretation of the Law differs from one's own," as Joel Marcus has so sharply put it.[19] There is a story of the nineteenth-century Rabbi Mendel of Kotzk (the famous Kotzker Rebbe) who said that many Jews concern themselves more with a blood spot on an egg than a blood spot on a ruble, but surely he himself remained just as careful about blood spots on eggs and expected no less from his followers "and all the Jews." (Recently Marcus has re-cited the Kotzker's apophthegm in precisely this Markan context.) Jesus' homily is indeed in this radically critical Jewish tradition that began with the great prophets and continued for millennia.

Let me repeat some verses from the text:

[14]Then he called the crowd again and said to them, "Listen to me, all of you, and understand: [15]there is nothing outside a person that by going in can defile, but the things that come out are what defile." [16, 17]When he had left the crowd and entered the house, his disciples asked him about the parable. [18]He said to them, "Then do you also fail to understand? Do you not see that whatever goes into a person from outside cannot defile, [19]since it enters,

not the heart but the stomach, and goes out into the sewer?" (Thus he declared all foods clean.) [20]And he said, "It is what comes out of a person that defiles. [21]For it is from within, from the human heart, that evil intentions come: fornication, theft, murder, [22]adultery, avarice, wickedness, deceit, licentiousness, envy, slander, pride, folly. [23]All these evil things come from within, and they defile a person."

Attentive readers will have noticed that verse 16 has been left out of my translation of the text, as it is in many standard versions. It is usually considered a later addition to the text, but actually it is original and the key to understanding the passage. It reads: "Let those who have ears, hear!" thus signaling that Jesus' statement about the law of purity is a parable, that the law itself has a deeper meaning. But the disciples could not understand the deeper meaning that Jesus' words were meant to convey. And so they asked him to explain. What, teacher, did you mean to teach us with this parable? And Jesus answered them: "Why does the Torah only render impure that which comes out and not that which goes in, if not to teach us something, namely, that morality is more important than the purity rules—and especially allegedly Pharisaic extensions of them?" This has absolutely nothing to do with abrogating the Law; it is just putting it in its place. The explanation that Jesus gives is to interpret the deep meaning of the Torah's rules, not to set them aside. And it is this deep interpretation of the Law that constitutes Jesus' great contribution—not an alleged rejection of the Law at all. Not an exhortation, then, to abandon the Torah, but a call to deepen our genuine commitment both to practicing it and to incorporating its meanings, Jesus' famous saying can be seen as entirely within a Jewish spiritual world.

When Jesus explains the parable to his uncomprehending disciples, he is showing how the literal force of the halakha itself should be read as indicating its spiritual or moral meaning.[20] Indeed, it is not what goes into the mouth that renders one impure but the impure intentions of a heart, as signified by the halakhic fact that things that go out of the body cause impurity. As I have mentioned above, all of the practices to which Jesus refers as pharisaic—the hand washing, the washing of vessels—are closely connected with the particular traditions of the Pharisees regarding the encroachment of impure foods on the purity of the body. Those Pharisees who believe that impurity (literal, halakhic impurity) comes from without miss entirely the spiritual import of the Torah's rule about impurity coming from within. In other words, Jesus' complaint against them is not a trivial point about unnecessary stringencies (whatever some think, he was not a liberal preacher-teacher) but a vitally important point about the interpretation of the halakha, which in his view the Pharisees have completely distorted, abandoning the Torah here as well as in the other example given (the support of parents). What Jesus argues is that when the Pharisees misunderstand the law and change it to allow impurity from outside in accord with their tradition, they are also revealing that they don't hear the law at all. They only read from outside and ignore the inner meaning, just as they add external impurity. The halakhic issue is thus a perfect little parable. When Jesus speaks of the purity or impurity of foods, he is not speaking about the kosher system at all, but about the pharisaic understanding of purity practices. Neither Jesus nor the evangelist held, suggested, or implied that the new Jesus movement constituted a step out to form a new religion.

Jesus as a thinker and teacher was, like all thinkers and teachers, part and parcel of a particular historical and cultural context, within which he did his creative religious work and intervened his interventions. His context was the Palestinian Judaism of the north of Palestine (Galilee) in the first century and its religious practices, ideas, and controversies, including controversies with Jewish teachers from other places, such as Jerusalem. Reading the Gospel of Mark in its fullest context suggests that here Jesus speaks from the position of a traditional Galilean Jew, one whose community and traditional practices are being criticized and interfered with from outside, that is, from Jerusalem, by the Judaeans (as is emphasized in the opening sentence of the story itself).[21] Jesus accuses these

Pharisees of introducing practices that are beyond what is written in the Torah, or even against what is written in the Torah, and fights against their so-called tradition of the elders (κατὰ τὴν παράδοσιν τῶν πρεσβυτέρων), which they take to be as important as the Torah, or sometimes, in the eyes of their opponents such as Jesus, as uprooting or superseding the Torah.[22] I would assert, moreover, that Jesus' Galilean disciples were following their own accepted traditional practice in their refusal of the (nonbiblical) notion that impure foods could render the body impure and hence their refusal to wash their hands before eating. Jesus' disciples are upbraided by these upstarts from Jerusalem for not observing the purity strictures that they had introduced and demanded on the basis of the "traditions of the elders." Jesus responds vigorously, accusing them of hypocrisy and of ascribing to their own rulings and practices an importance greater than that of the Torah. There is thus nothing in Mark's version of this passage, let alone Matthew's, that suggests that Jesus is calling for abandoning the Torah at all. The Galileans were antipathetic to the urban Judaean/Jerusalemite pharisaic innovations.[23]

When put into its historical context, the chapter is perfectly clear. Mark was a Jew and his Jesus kept kosher. At least in its attitude toward the embodied practices of the Torah, Mark's Gospel does not in any way constitute even a baby step in the direction of the invention of

Christianity as a new religion or as a departure from Judaism at all.[24]

Mark is best read as a Jewish text, even in its most radical Christological moments. Nothing that Mark's Jesus proposes or argues for or enacts would have been inappropriate for a thoroughly Jewish Messiah, the Son of Man, and what would later be called Christianity is a brilliantly successful—the most brilliantly successful—Jewish apocalyptic and messianic movement. In his now-classic book *The Ghost Dance: The Origins of Religion*, Weston La Barre has the following to say about Christianity: "Indeed, to take a firmly secular view of it, Christianity itself was a crisis cult. Initially it was an ordinary politico-military revolt in the traditional Hebrew mold of secular messiahs, one of whom the Roman governor Pilate straightforwardly regarded as a rebellious would-be King of the Jews of the Davidic line, and executed in a usual fashion."[25] He follows this "firmly secular" account with a further story about how the Jews never would have thought of a "supernatural Hellenistic Messiah," and that the idea of the dying and resurrected Jesus could only have come in via "a Neolithic vegetation spirit, the 'dying god' of the Near East." Even from a purely historical point of view, this account, cited here as typical of so many, can have no purchase, as it totally ignores the *Jewish* history of the divine, "supernatural" Redeemer that we have been exploring throughout this book so far. La Barre, oddly enough, writes about Daniel 7 as also being the record of a "crisis cult" but then seems to totally ignore or deny the connections of that ancient text with any later development within Judaism. In the next and final chapter of this book, I'm going to make a case that even the suffering and death of the Messiah can plausibly be traced to the Jewish environment of Mark and his Jesus and, I suggest, to their own further reading of Daniel 7, and that in any case such an idea was hardly foreign to the Jewish imagination.

4

The Suffering Christ as a Midrash on Daniel

THE SUFFERING JESUS ON HIS CROSS may be in some ways the central, defining image of Christianity, and even Christendom for most of us. Christians wear the cross, and they cross themselves. For centuries, artists have depicted the scene of the suffering Messiah myriad times; in modernity, even Jewish artists such as Chagall have represented this iconic Christian emblem. Over and over again, we find the commonplace (and commonsense) statement that what divides Christians and Jews most sharply is the idea that the divine Messiah could suffer and die; indeed, many hold that it was this belief (produced, supposedly, after the fact) that was the most tangible marker of an absolute break between Jews and their new rivals, the Christians. In his now near-classic statement of the absolute difference of Jewish from Christian ideas of the Messiah, *The*

Messianic Idea in Israel, Joseph Klausner, the important Jewish historian of the Second Temple, makes the following argument, or rather, offers the absolutely dominant and prevailing view of this matter: that initially the only difference between "Christians" and "Jews" was that the former believed that the Messiah had already come while the latter believed that he was yet to come:[1]

> But because of the fact that the Messiah who had already come was crucified as an ordinary rebel after being scourged and humiliated, and thus was not successful in the political sense, having failed to redeem his people Israel; because of the lowly political status of the Jews at the end of the period of the Second Temple and after the Destruction; and because of the fear that the Romans would persecute believers in a political Messiah, for these reasons there perforce came about a development of ideas, which after centuries of controversy became crystallized in Christianity.[2]

According to Klausner's generally held view, the idea of messianic suffering, death, and resurrection came about only as an apology after the fact of Jesus' death. In this view, it is simply a scandal for Christian messianic thought that Jesus was scourged and humiliated as a common rebel, despite the fact that he was the Messiah. In that case, "then why did God allow His Chosen One, the Messiah, to undergo frightful suffering and even to be crucified the most shameful death of all, according to Cicero 24 and Tacitus 2B and not save him from all these things? The answer can only be that it was the will of God and the will of the Messiah himself that he should be scourged, humiliated, and crucified. But whence came a purpose like this, that would bring about suffering and death without sin?"[3] The answer to the question of Jesus' suffering and death, according to Klausner (and nearly everyone else), is that the suffering of the Messiah was vicarious and the death an atoning death—in other words, the common Christian theology of the cross. After the Messiah Jesus' humiliation, suffering, and death, according to this view—held by many Christian thinkers and scholars as well as Jewish ones—the theology of Jesus' redemptive, vicarious suffering was discovered, as it were, in Isaiah 53, which was allegedly reinterpreted as referring not to the persecuted People of Israel, but to the suffering Messiah:

[10]Yet it was the will of the Lord to crush him with pain. When you make his life an offering for sin, he shall see his offspring, and shall prolong his days; through him the will of the Lord shall prosper. [11]Out of his anguish he shall see light; he shall find satisfaction through his knowledge. The righteous one, my servant, shall make many righteous, and he shall bear their iniquities. [12]Therefore I will allot

him a portion with the great, and he shall divide the
spoil with the strong; because he poured out himself
to death, and was numbered with the transgressors;
yet he bore the sin of many, and made intercession
for the transgressors.

If these verses do indeed refer to the Messiah, they
clearly predict his suffering and death to atone for the
sins of humans, but the Jews allegedly always interpreted
these verses as referring to the suffering of Israel herself
and not the Messiah, who would only triumph. To sum up
this generally held view: The theology of the suffering of
the Messiah was an after-the-fact apologetic response to
explain the suffering and ignominy Jesus suffered, since
he was deemed by "Christians" to be the Messiah. Christianity, on this view, was initiated by the fact of the crucifixion, which is seen as setting into motion the new religion.
Moreover, many who hold this view hold also that Isaiah 53 was distorted by the Christians from its allegedly
original meaning, in which it referred to the suffering of
the People of Israel, to explain and account for the shocking fact that the Messiah had been crucified.

This commonplace view has to be rejected completely.
The notion of the humiliated and suffering Messiah was
not at all alien within Judaism before Jesus' advent, and it
remained current among Jews well into the future following that—indeed, well into the early modern period.[4] The

fascinating (and to some, no doubt, uncomfortable) fact is that this tradition was well documented by modern Messianic Jews, who are concerned to demonstrate that their belief in Jesus does not make them un-Jewish. Whether or not one accepts their theology, it remains the case that they have a very strong textual base for the view that the suffering Messiah is based in deeply rooted Jewish texts early and late. Jews, it seems, had no difficulty whatever with understanding a Messiah who would vicariously suffer to redeem the world. Once again, what has been allegedly ascribed to Jesus after the fact is, in fact, a piece of entrenched messianic speculation and expectation that was current before Jesus came into the world at all. That the Messiah would suffer and be humiliated was something Jews learned from close reading of the biblical texts, a close reading in precisely the style of classically rabbinic interpretation that has become known as midrash, the concordance of verses and passages from different places in Scripture to derive new narratives, images, and theological ideas.

Throughout this book, we have been observing how ideas that have been thought to be the most distinctive innovations of Jesus himself or his followers can be found in the religious literature of the Jews of the time of Jesus or before. This observation takes nothing away from the dignity or majesty of the Christian story, nor is it meant to. Rather than seeing Christianity as a new invention, seeing it as one of the paths that Judaism took—a path as ancient in its sources as the one that rabbinic Jews trod—has a majesty of its own. Many Jews were expecting the divine-human Messiah, the Son of Man. Many accepted Jesus as that figure, while others did not. Although there is precious little pre-Christian evidence among Jews for the suffering of the Messiah, there are good reasons to consider this too no stumbling block for the "Jewishness" of the ideas about the Messiah, Jesus as well. Let me make clear I am not claiming that Jesus and his followers contributed nothing new to the story of a suffering and dying Messiah; I am not, of course, denying them their own religious creativity. I am claiming that even this innovation, if indeed they innovated, was entirely within the spirit and hermeneutical method of ancient Judaism, and not a scandalous departure from it.

This point of the "Jewishness" of the vicarious sufferings of the Messiah can be established in two ways: first by showing how the Gospels use perfectly traditional, midrashic ways of reasoning to develop these ideas and apply them to Jesus, and second, by demonstrating how common the idea of a suffering and dying Messiah was among perfectly "orthodox" rabbinic Jews from the time of the Talmud and onward. My reasoning is that if this were such a shocking thought, how is it that the rabbis of the Talmud and midrash, only a couple of centuries later, had no difficulty whatever with portraying the Messiah's vicarious

suffering or discovering him in Isaiah 53, just as the followers of Jesus had done?[5] But I get ahead of myself: first,
let us see how close biblical reading in the style of midrash
can best explain the passages in Mark that speak of the
shaming and death of Jesus.

Shaming the Son of Man: Mark 8:38

The first time in Mark that Jesus reveals the inevitability
of his suffering and death is in chapter 8. As we have seen,
the sometimes puzzling and shocking statements made by
Jesus about his authority can be derived from close reading of the Daniel passages about the Son of Man. These
Jews pored over the Scripture and interpreted every detail
in order to understand what the Messiah would look like
and what to expect when he came. Here we have a further
example that illuminates our question about the suffering
of the Messiah:

> [27]And Jesus went with his disciples, to the villages
> of Caesarea Philippi; and on the way he asked his
> disciples, "Who do men say that I am?" [28]And they
> told him, "John the Baptist; and others say, Elijah;
> and others one of the prophets." [29]And he asked
> them, "But who do you say I am?" Peter answered
> him, "You are the Christ." [30]And he charged them
> to tell no one about him. [31]And he began to teach

them that the Son of man must suffer many things, and be rejected by the elders and the chief priests and the scribes, and be killed, and after three days rise again. [32]And he said this plainly. And Peter took him, and began to rebuke him. [33]But turning and seeing his disciples, he rebuked Peter, and said, "Get thee behind me Satan! For you are not on the side of God, but of men." [34]And he called to him the multitude with his disciples, and said to them, "If any man would come after me, let him deny himself and take up his cross and follow me. [35]For whoever would save his life will lose it; and whoever loses his life for my sake and the gospel's will save it. [36]For what does it profit a man, to gain the whole world and forfeit his life? [37]For what can a man give in return for his life? [38]*For whoever is ashamed of me and of my words in this adulterous and sinful generation, of him will the Son of Man also be ashamed, when he comes in the glory of his Father with the holy angels.*

In this passage, as in the immediately following Mark 9:12, we are told by Jesus that the Son of Man must "suffer many things." In the sequence of vv. 29–31 it is made absolutely clear that the Christ will suffer and that Jesus believes that he is the Christ. The equation of the Son of Man and his suffering with the Christ is made absolutely clear in these verses as well. This all makes the most sense if we assume that Jesus is alluding to the Son of Man figure from Daniel and his fate, which is to be crushed for a time, two times, and half a time before rising triumphant.

Jesus had a very clear sense of his messianic role and fate, and that this role and fate were what had been predicted for the Son of Man in Daniel 7. Jesus first is identified as Messiah by others and then refers to himself as the Son of Man, thus establishing the identity of the Messiah and his ultimate fate as that of the Danielic Son of Man. Jesus is also clearly claiming that identity for himself.

In Mark 14:62, we find a similar, and if anything even more explicit, self-identification by Jesus as Messiah and Son of Man. It would be no exaggeration to say that these two explicit moments in which this equation is made provide a key to reading all of the Son of Man passages in the Gospel as indicating Jesus' sense of his divine vocation and role:

> "Are you the Christ, the son of the Blessed One?" And Jesus said "I am, and you will see the Son of Man seated at the right hand of Power, and coming on the clouds of Heaven." Then the high priest tore his clothes and said, "Why do we still need witnesses? You have heard his blasphemy!"

We learn several key things from this passage.[6] The first, as we saw above, is that "Messiah" is for Jesus equivalent to the "Son of Man." Second, we learn that claiming to be the Son of Man was considered blasphemy by the high priest and thus a claim not only to messianic status but also to divinity. When Jesus answers "I am," he is going even further than merely claiming messianic status, for "I Am," *eigo eimi*, is precisely what YHVH calls himself when Moses asks his name: "This is what you are to say to the Israelites, 'I am [*eigo eimi*] has sent me to you' " (Exodus 3:14). The high priest of the Jews could hardly be expected to miss this allusion. Jesus claims to be the Son of God, the Son of Man, and indeed God himself. A statement such as that is not merely true or false; it is truth or blasphemy.* It is also the same blasphemy of which Jesus

---

* According to the Mishna, Sanhedrin 7:5, it is mentioning the name of God that constitutes blasphemy. Both Josephus and the Community Rule of Qumran precede the Mishna in this determination. I contend, therefore, that it is most plausible to understand Jesus' "I Am" as being the name of God, hence the blasphemy. Many scholars deny this argument, contending that "I Am" is merely a declarative sentence and not a predication of the name of God to himself (see Adela Yarbro Collins, *Mark: A Commentary*, ed. Harold W. Attridge, Hermeneia—a Critical and Historical Commentary on the Bible [Minneapolis, MN: Fortress Press, 2007], 704–6). The blasphemy, then, has to be understood differently, namely, in connection with Philo's definition of blasphemy, which is, as she says, somewhat less stringent than that of the Mishna, Josephus, or Qumran (see Adela Yarbro Collins, "The Charge of Blasphemy in Mark 14:64," *Journal for the Study of the New Testament* 26, 4 [2004]: 379–401). In my view, an interpretation of the text that is closest to the other Palestinian views of the matter is preferable, but Yarbro Collins may, of course, be right. In support of her view is the verse in Mark 2 discussed above where Jesus is accused of blasphemy for having arrogated to himself the divine prerogative to forgive sins. However, even on Philo's account, blasphemy

was accused in chapter 2, when he presumed the divine prerogative of forgiving sins. Third, we learn that for the Jesus of the Gospels, the title "Son of Man" derives from Daniel 7, is the name for the divine redeemer of a high Christology, and thus constitutes the blasphemy of which the high priest speaks.

The high priest clearly knows the terms "Christ," "Son of God," and "Son of Man." He also perceives that when Jesus says "I am," he is declaring himself the one whose name is "I am," YHVH himself. Through all of these terms, Jesus is claiming some share of divinity, hence the charge of blasphemy.[7] Here it cannot be denied, of course, that

---

consists of imputing divine status to oneself or to another human, so my point that the blasphemy consists precisely in Jesus claiming divine status for himself stands. Even if *eigo eimi* is innocent, Jesus' further allusion to himself as the Son of Man and coming with the clouds of heaven certainly, according to the high priest's reaction, constitutes blasphemy and thus a claim to divine status. Compare also John 8:57–58: "Then the Jews said to him, 'You are not yet fifty years old and you have seen Abraham?' He said to them, 'Truly, truly I say until you, before Abraham came into being, I Am [*eigo eimi*].' They then picked up stones that they might cast them at him." This is precisely the same as what happens here in Mark. Jesus in both Gospels is understood as claiming divine status through naming himself as YHVH names himself. Since stoning is the biblically ordained punishment for blasphemy, the people seek to stone him. This is precisely the same blasphemy for which Stephen was stoned according to Acts 7:56, although there the blasphemy consisted in implying the divine status of Jesus, not, of course, his own. To my knowledge, this is the only place in which "Son of Man" is used of Jesus by someone other than Jesus himself; it shows how charged was the claim to be the Son of Man, which only makes sense if it is a claim to divinity.

there is a direct allusion to the Danielic source of the narrative of the Son of Man, which is explicitly signaled by the words "coming with the clouds of heavens"; thus I suggest the parallel provides good evidence for my interpretation of the Mark 8 passage as well. As in 14:62, he refers to the exaltation of the Son of Man; in 8:31 he refers to the suffering and humiliation of the Son of Man, which is then cited again in 9:12, "as it has been written." The two verses thus complete each other.

The progression of the Gospel narrative runs in the following fashion:

- Jesus asks the disciples who they think he is.
- Peter answers that he is the Messiah.
- Jesus answers that the Son of Man must suffer many things.
- Peter denies this (he is ashamed of a suffering Messiah).
- Jesus rebukes him.
- Jesus calls the disciples together to provide them with the lesson to be learned from his sharp rebuke of Peter.
- All who would be followers of Jesus must pick up crosses and be willing to lose their lives as he will.
- But if any are ashamed of Jesus in his humiliation and crucifixion, the exalted Son of Man (Jesus vindicated) will be ashamed of them in

the final moment, when he comes in glory with
his angels (Daniel 7).[8]

It is precisely under the title Son of Man that Jesus
predicates his sufferings. At the end of chapter 7 of Daniel,
the symbol of the Son of Man is interpreted as "the People
of the Saints of the Most High," who will be crushed for a
certain amount of time under the heels of the fourth beast
and then will arise and, defeating the beast, "will receive
the kingdom and hold the kingdom forever and ever."[9] It
surely can hardly be doubted that the phrase "the Son of
Man must suffer many things, and be rejected" is a pal-
pable allusion to Isaiah 53:3, in which we are told that the
suffering servant of the Lord "is despised and rejected of
men." This, as we have seen, is very plausibly read about
the Messiah. We must also, of course, be mindful of other
biblical texts in the background here, including especially
the psalms of lament. We therefore don't need to posit
a special Christian mode of reading that led to this idea.
Once again, the primary mode of early Jewish biblical
exegesis is midrash, which is the concatenation of related
(or even seemingly unrelated) passages and verses from
all over the Bible to derive new lessons and narratives. It is
midrash that we see at work here too.

The association of these prophetic texts with the Son
of Man from Daniel is precisely what enabled the full development of a suffering Christology, according to which

Jesus' demise (and exaltation) was interpreted. In other words, it is as plausible to assume that Jews held this view of the vicarious suffering of the Messiah and his atoning death, as predicted by the Prophet Isaiah before Jesus' own suffering and death, as it is to assume that Christians made it up after the fact. Once again, we find a Jesus who sees himself, imagines himself, and presents himself as entirely fulfilling the messianic expectation already in place to the effect that the "Son of Man must suffer many things."

The Jews were expecting a Redeemer in the time of Jesus. Their own sufferings under Roman domination seemed so great, and this Redeemer had been predicted for them. Reading the Book of Daniel closely, at least some Jews—those behind the first-century Similitudes of Enoch and those with Jesus—had concluded that the Redeemer would be a divine figure named the Son of Man who would come to earth as a human, save the Jews from oppression, and rule the world as its sovereign. Jesus seemed to many to fit that bill. His life and death were claimed to be precisely a fulfillment of what had been predicted of the Messiah, Son of Man, by the old books and traditions. What happened as that expectation of redemption was delayed and as more Gentiles joined this community is the story of the Church, of Christianity. It is not the suffering and dying of the Messiah that precipitated that story at all, as we see once we read the Gospel in its close connection to Daniel.

The connection with Daniel may be even clearer when we look at the parallel version of this teaching of Jesus to the disciples in 9:31:

> [30]They went on from there and passed through Galilee. And he would not have any one know it; [31]for he was teaching his disciples, saying to them, "The Son of man will be delivered into the hands of men, and they will kill him; and when he is killed, after three days he will rise." [32]But they did not understand the saying, and they were afraid to ask him.

That this enmity will arise against the Messiah can also clearly be derived by midrashic reading of the end of Daniel 7 as well:

> [25]And he will speak words against the Most High, and he will oppress the high holy ones, and he will think to change the times and the law, and they will be delivered into his hand until a time, two times, and half a time. [26]But the judgment shall sit, and they shall take away his dominion, to consume and to destroy it unto the end. [27]And the kingdom and the dominion, and the greatness of the kingdoms under the whole heaven, shall be given to the people

of the saints of the Most High: his kingdom is an everlasting kingdom, and all dominions shall serve and obey him.

Those Jews who read the Son of Man in accord with the end of the chapter as representing the People of Israel had to do some harmonizing work to explain away the clearly divine implications of the vision in the first part, but those Jews, in turn, who gloried in the divinity of the Son of Man also had some hard harmonizing work to do to explain the end of the chapter in accordance with their reading of the first part, understanding the "People of the Most High" as that divine Messiah. It is the Christ, Jesus, who is accordingly handed over to the wicked one for a prescribed interval, here said to be "a time, two times, and half a time." This narrative of the Messiah was not a revolutionary departure within the religious history of the communities of readers of the Bible but an obvious and plausible consequence of a well-established tradition of reading Daniel 7 as being about a divine-human Messiah.[10] Jesus' resurrection "after three days," according to the Markan version, as opposed to the "in three days" of the later evangelists, could possibly derive as well from a close reading of the Daniel passage, for if Jesus' suffering before exaltation comes from the "time, two times, and half a time" during which the one like a Son of Man is to suffer in Daniel 7, and if these "times" are understood as days, then Jesus would rise after a day, two more days, and part of a day, that is, after the third day. But this must remain a speculation.

"As It Is Written Concerning Him": Mark 9:11–13

Jesus' story and his progressive self-revelation to his disciples return again and again to Scripture—and to midrash on that Scripture. Mark 9:11–13 is the account of Jesus' conversation with his disciples after the transfiguration on the mountain. It thus represents a highly emphasized climactic moment in the story of the Gospel and one that is particularly telling for Christology. This passage has puzzled most commentators till now, but we will see that the text is best understood as part and parcel of a Jewish tradition of the suffering Messiah. Here are the verses in their necessary and immediate context, following the transfiguration in which Moses, Elijah, and Jesus have been revealed to be close associates (at the very least) in a vision:

> [9]As they were coming down the mountain, he ordered them to tell no one about what they had seen, until after the Son of Man had risen from the dead. [10]So they kept the matter to themselves, questioning what this rising from the dead could mean. [11]And they asked him saying, Why do the scribes say that Elijah must come first? [12]And he said to them, Elijah

when he comes first restores all things. And how has it been written of the Son of Man that he should suffer many things and be rejected?[11] [13]But I say to you that Elijah has come and they did to him whatever they wanted, as has been written concerning him.

As many commentators have written, this passage raises great difficulties. There is no record in the Scriptures that Elijah would be mistreated, so on what basis does the Gospel read that "it has been written concerning him"?[12] Further, as Joel Marcus has pointed out, "if Elijah restores all things, then how once conceive of a Messiah who is to be rejected by humanity, a Messiah whose suffering and rejection are foretold in the scripture (9:12c)? The two expectations appear to contradict each other."[13] Marcus's brilliant move here is to realize that this is not a flaw in the Gospel text but its very vocation.[14] This contradiction is what the Gospel text is about; this is not a "bug," as we might say, but a feature. We have something very close to a standard midrashic form here: the question of the disciples is not "How is it written that Elijah will come first?" but "Why do the scribes say this, for if what they say is true: How is it written that the Son of Man will suffer many things?" They are pointing to a contradiction between the verse to which Jesus refers and the statements of the scribes, not between two verses.[15]

The disciples understand Jesus of vv. 9–11 very well. They understand that what has been revealed to them is that Jesus is the Son of Man, and they know what that means. They are astounded, as they always are, that Jesus will suffer, even though, as Jesus points out, it is, indeed, written that the Son of Man will suffer. After all, at the end of the chapter in 9:30, they still have not understood Jesus' prediction that he will be handed over to human beings, that they will kill him, and that he will rise. They are also puzzled that Jesus as the Messiah has come but Elijah seemingly hasn't, and the scribes say that Elijah will come before the Messiah and restore all things.

Jesus' answer is brilliantly to the point:

> [11]And they asked him saying, Why do the scribes say that Elijah must come first? [12]And he said to them, Elijah when he comes first restores all things. And how has it been written of the Son of Man that he should suffer many things and be rejected? [13]But I say to you that Elijah has come and they did to him whatever they wanted, as has been written concerning him.

The *Scribes* say that Elijah, coming before the Son of Man, will restore all things and thus how could it be that the Son of Man will suffer? And Jesus answers: Does the

Prophet, in fact, say that Elijah will restore all things; if that were the case, how, indeed, could it be written that the Son of Man will suffer many things? No, Jesus maintains (correctly), it does not say in the verse that Elijah will restore all things; it is the Scribes who came up with this idea themselves. And the Scribes must simply be wrong in their interpretation of the coming of Elijah; all will be restored, not by Elijah but by the Son of Man and only after the terrible sufferings of the Day of the Lord, which are themselves written clearly in the text of Malakhi. Now the answer is clear: Elijah has come already in the form of John the Baptist (as explicitly in Matthew), the forerunner, and they did to him what they wished to.[16] His suffering becomes a type of the suffering that the Son of Man also will undergo, and the disciples are answered in both of their questions. Jesus is shown here, as also in the halakhic discussions that we have encountered previously, besting the Scribes and the Pharisees at their own game of midrash. The idea of the suffering of the Son of Man is anything but an alien import into Judaism; in fact, it is its very vocation.

It is here perhaps more than anywhere else in the Gospel of Mark that we see its background in the Jewish mode of biblical interpretation, midrash. Once again, to remind readers, midrash is a way to multiply contextualizing verses with other verses and passages in the Bible,

in order to determine their meaning. Our passage here
is quite close in form to a type of tannaitic midrash in
which a verse is cited, a commentary is offered, another
contradictory verse is cited, and the first comment is either revised or rejected.[17] This argument would strongly
support the claim that the Gospels, or at least this Gospel, are working in something very close to a midrashic
mode for the generation of their narrative, especially for
the present purposes in anything having to do with the
Son of Man. Once again, we see here evidence that the
idea of a suffering Messiah would not have been at all foreign to Jewish sensibilities, which derived their very messianic hopes and expectations from such methods of close
reading of Scripture, just as Jesus did. This identification
between the Son of Man and the fate of Jesus comes to
its culmination in the verses from chapter 14 (discussed
above) in which Jesus is asked about his messianic identity by the high priests just before the crucifixion and confesses openly (for the first time) that he is the Son of God,
the Messiah, the Son of Man who will come on the clouds
of heaven.

Isaiah's "Suffering Servant" as Messiah in Jewish Traditions

The suffering Messiah who atones for our sins was a familiar idea throughout the history of the Jewish religion, even long after there truly was a separation from Christianity. The idea of a suffering Messiah is present in ancient, medieval, and early modern Judaism. This fact, at the very least, calls into question the truism that the formation and acceptance of this idea by followers of Jesus constituted the necessary and absolute breaking point with the religion of Israel. The Suffering Messiah is part and parcel of Jewish tradition from antiquity to modernity. Not only, then, is the Gospel drawing on Jewish tradition but this idea remained a Jewish one long after Christianity had indeed been separated off in late antiquity.

One of many important pieces of evidence for this view is this history of how Jewish commentators have interpreted Isaiah 53:

> Who has believed what we have heard? And to whom has the arm of the Lord been revealed? [2]For he grew up before him like a young plant, and like a root out of dry ground; he had no form or majesty that we should look at him, nothing in his appearance that we should desire him. [3]He was despised and rejected by others; a man of suffering and

acquainted with infirmity; and as one from whom others hide their faces he was despised, and we held him of no account.

⁴Surely he has borne our infirmities and carried our diseases; yet we accounted him stricken, struck down by God, and afflicted. ⁵But he was wounded for our transgressions, crushed for our iniquities; upon him was the punishment that made us whole, and by his bruises we are healed. ⁶All we like sheep have gone astray; we have all turned to our own way, and the Lord has laid on him the iniquity of us all. ⁷He was oppressed, and he was afflicted, yet he did not open his mouth; like a lamb that is led to the slaughter, and like a sheep that before its shearers is silent, so he did not open his mouth. ⁸By a perversion of justice he was taken away. Who could have imagined his future? For he was cut off from the land of the living, stricken for the transgression of my people. ⁹They made his grave with the wicked and his tomb with the rich, although he had done no violence, and there was no deceit in his mouth.

¹⁰Yet it was the will of the Lord to crush him with pain. When you make his life an offering for sin, he shall see his offspring, and shall prolong his days; through him the will of the Lord shall prosper. ¹¹Out of his anguish he shall see light; he shall find satisfaction through his knowledge. The righteous one, my servant, shall make many righteous, and

he shall bear their iniquities. ¹²Therefore I will allot him a portion with the great, and he shall divide the spoil with the strong; because he poured out himself to death, and was numbered with the transgressors; yet he bore the sin of many, and made intercession for the transgressors.

I cannot overstate the extent to which the interpretation of this passage has anchored the conventional view of Judaism's relationship to Messianism. It has been generally assumed by modern folks that Jews have always given the passage a metaphorical reading, understanding the suffering servant to refer to the People of Israel, and that it was the Christians who changed and distorted its meaning to make it refer to Jesus. Quite to the contrary, we now know that many Jewish authorities, maybe even most, until nearly the modern period have read Isaiah 53 as being about the Messiah; until the last few centuries, the allegorical reading was a minority position.

Aside from one very important—but absolutely unique—notice in Origen's *Contra Celsum*, there is no evidence at all that any late ancient Jews read Isaiah 52–53 as referring to anyone but the Messiah.[18] There are, on the other hand, several attestations of ancient rabbinic readings of the song as concerning the Messiah and his tribulations.

The Palestinian Talmud, commenting on the biblical

passage "And the land shall mourn" (Zechariah 12:12), cites two amoraic opinions: one amora who interprets "This is the mourning over the Messiah" and one who disagrees, arguing that it is the mourning over the sexual desire (that has been killed in the messianic age) (PT Sukkah 5:2 55b).[19] There are, moreover, traditions in the Babylonian Talmud and thus attested from the fourth to the sixth centuries A.D. (but very likely earlier), the most famous and explicit of which is Sanhedrin 98b. Referring to the Messiah, the Talmud asks there openly, "What is his name?" and various names are proffered by different rabbis. After several different views, we find: "And the Rabbis say, 'the leper' of the House of Rabbi is his name, for it says, 'Behold he has borne our disease,[20] and suffered our pains, and we thought him smitten, beaten by God and tortured' [Isa. 53:4]." We see here both the vicarious suffering of the Messiah and the use of Isaiah 53 to anchor the idea. This midrash (or one very like it) is what lies behind the heartrending image that appears only one page earlier in the Talmud of the Messiah sitting at the gates of Rome among the poor and those who suffer from painful disease. They all loosen and bind their bandages at one time, and he loosens and binds them one at a time, saying: "Perhaps I will be needed and I don't want to delay." Thus the Messiah too, ever mindful of his soteriological mission, suffers from the same disease and painful tortures of the indigent and sick of Rome.

Another classical rabbinic passage might perhaps be the earliest attestation from the tradition: [21]

Rabbi Yose Hagelili said: Go forth and learn the praise of the King Messiah and the reward of the righteous from the First Adam. For he was only commanded one thou-shalt-not commandment and he violated it. Behold how many deaths he and his descendants and the descendants of his descendants were fined until the end of all of the generations. Now which of God's qualities is greater than the other, the quality of mercy or the quality of retribution? Proclaim that the quality of goodness is the greater and the quality of retribution the lesser! And the King Messiah fasts and suffers for the sinners, as it says, "and he is made sick for our sins etc." ever more so and more will he be triumphant for all of the generations, as it says, "And the Lord visited upon him the sin of all." [22]

If this text be deemed genuine, then we have clear evidence that by the third century, rabbinic readers understood the suffering servant to be the Messiah who suffers to vicariously atone for the sins of humans.

There are also various medieval Jewish commentators, among them figures marginal to rabbinic Judaism (but hardly suspected of Christian leanings) such as the

Karaite Yefet ben Ali, who clearly understand the Isaiah text and its suffering servant as about the Messiah.[23] The early modern Kabbalist Rabbi Moshe Alshekh, also a spotlessly "orthodox" rabbinite teacher, writes, "I may remark, then, that our Rabbis with one voice accept and affirm the opinion that the prophet is speaking of the King Messiah, and we ourselves also adhere to the same view."[24] The intellectual giant of Spanish Jewry, Rabbi Moses ben Nahman, concedes that according to the midrash and the rabbis of the Talmud, Isaiah 53 is entirely about the Messiah, but he dissents.[25]

As we see, neither Judaism nor Jews have ever spoken with one voice on this (hermeneutical) theological question, and therefore there is no sense in which the assertion of many sufferings and rejection and contempt for the Son of Man constitutes a break with Judaism or the religion of Israel. Indeed, in the Gospels these ideas have been derived from the Torah (Scripture in its broadest meaning) by that most Jewish of exegetical styles, the way of midrash.[26] There is no essentially Christian (drawn from the cross) versus Jewish (triumphalist) notion of the Messiah, but only one complex and contested messianic idea, shared by Mark and Jesus with the full community of the Jews. The description of the Christ as predicting his own suffering and then that very suffering in the Passion narrative, the Passion of the Christ, does not in any way then contradict the assertion of Martin Hengel that "Christianity grew *entirely* out of Jewish soil."[27]

Gospel Judaism was straightforwardly and completely a Jewish-messianic movement, and the Gospel the story of the Jewish Christ.

Epilogue

The Jewish Gospel

JEWS NOT INFREQUENTLY ARGUE THAT Christianity appropriated the Hebrew Bible and turned it to its own non-Jewish purposes, thus distorting its meanings. This book challenges this claim in two ways. On one hand, the implication of my argument is that Christianity hijacked not only the Old Testament but the New Testament as well by turning that thoroughly Jewish text away from its cultural origins among the Jewish communities of Palestine in the first century and making it an attack on the traditions of the Jews, traditions that, I maintain, it sought to uphold and not destroy, traditions that give the narrative its richest literary and hermeneutical context. On the other hand, this book challenges the notion that the New Testament itself is an appropriation, or—even better—a misappropriation of the Old. If the interpretations offered here hold water, then the New Testament is much more deeply embedded within Second Temple Jewish life and thought than many have imagined, even—and this I emphasize again—in the very moments that we take to be most characteristically Christian as opposed to Jewish: the notion of a dual godhead with a Father and a Son, the notion of a Redeemer who himself will be both God and man, and the notion that this Redeemer would suffer and die as part of the salvational process. At least some of these ideas, the Father/Son godhead and the suffering savior, have deep roots in the Hebrew Bible as well and may be among some of the most ancient ideas about God and the world that the Israelite people ever held.

Many, perhaps even most, New Testament scholars today argue that the most striking parts of the Jesus story as told in the Gospels—that he was the Messiah, the Son of Man; that he died and was resurrected; and that he is to be worshipped as God—all stem *ex eventu* (after the fact) from the earliest followers of Jesus, who developed these ideas in the wake of his death and their experiences of his resurrection appearances. Thus, one of the finest and most respected (by me, as well, of course) scholars of New Testament today, Adela Yarbro Collins, writes openly, "Most New Testament scholars would still agree with Bultmann's judgment that the creation of the 'idea of a suffering, dying, rising Messiah or Son of Man' was 'not done by Jesus himself but by' his followers '*ex eventu*,' that is, after the fact of the crucifixion and the experiences of Jesus as risen."[1] In this, she is, as she says, entirely representative of the dominant scholarly tradition today about the Son of Man and the exalted status of Jesus, the Christ. As it was recently put to me by an orthodox Jewish scholar of rabbinics, the Gospel story is a complete novelty engendered by the remarkable life and death of the man Jesus of Nazareth.

The historian in me rebels at such an account. Taking even the remarkable nature of Jesus—and I have no doubt that he *was* a remarkable person—as the historical explanation for a world-shifting revision of beliefs and practices seems to me hardly plausible. It may have been necessary that Jesus was so extraordinary for such a compelling narrative of divine being and function to have developed, but it was hardly sufficient. Even more so, the notion that some kind of experience of the risen Christ preceded and gave rise to the idea that he would rise seems to me so unlikely as to be incredible. Perhaps his followers saw him arisen, but surely this must be because they had a narrative that led them to expect such appearances, and not that the appearances gave rise to the narrative.* An alternative account such as I have given here seems much more likely to make historical sense. A people had been for centuries

---

* Let me make myself clear here: I am not denying the validity of the religious Christian view of matters. That is surely a matter of faith, not scholarship. I am denying it as a historical, scholarly, critical explanation.

talking about, thinking about, and reading about a new king, a son of David, who would come to redeem them from Seleucid and then Roman oppression, and they had come to think of that king as a second, younger, divine figure on the basis of the Book of Daniel's reflection of that very ancient tradition. So they were persuaded to see in Jesus of Nazareth the one whom they had expected to come: the Messiah, the Christ. A fairly ordinary story of a prophet, a magician, a charismatic teacher is thoroughly transformed when that teacher understands himself—or is understood by others—as this coming one. Details of his life, his prerogatives, his powers, and even his suffering and death before triumph are all developed out of close midrashic reading of the biblical materials and fulfilled in his life and death. The exaltation and resurrection experiences of his followers are a product of the narrative, not a cause of it. This is not to deny any creativity on the part of Jesus or his early or later followers, but only to suggest strongly that such creativity is most richly and compellingly read within the Jewish textual and intertextual world, the echo chamber of a Jewish soundscape of the first century.

Notes

Introduction

1. Paula Fredriksen, "Mandatory Retirement: Ideas in the Study of Christian Origins Whose Time Has Come to Go," in *Israel's God and Rebecca's Children: Christology and Community in Early Judaism and Christianity: Essays in Honor of Larry W. Hurtado and Alan F. Segal*, ed. David B. Capes et al. (Waco, TX: Baylor University Press, 2007), 25.
2. I will be developing this idea further in a forthcoming book, entitled *How the Jews Got Religion* (New York: Fordham University Press, 2013).
3. Shaye J.D. Cohen, "The Significance of Yavneh: Pharisees, Rabbis, and the End of Jewish Sectarianism," *Hebrew Union College Annual* 55 (1984): 27–53.
4. For one of the best historical descriptions of this process, see R.P.C. Hanson, *The Search for the Christian Doctrine of God: The Arian Controversy 318–381 AD* (Edinburgh: T & T Clark, 1988).
5. Robert L. Wilken, *John Chrysostom and the Jews: Rhetoric and Reality in the Late 4th Century* (Berkeley: University of California Press, 1983).
6. Jerome, *Correspondence*, ed. Isidorus Hilberg, Corpus Scriptorum Ecclesiasticorum Latinorum (Vienna: Verlag der Osterreichischen Akademie der Wissenschaften, 1996), 55:381–82 (my translation).
7. See also Reuven Kimelman, "Birkat Ha-Minim and the Lack of Evidence for an Anti-Christian Jewish Prayer in Late

Antiquity," in *Aspects of Judaism in the Greco-Roman Period*, vol. 2, *Jewish and Christian Self-Definition*, ed. E.P. Sanders, A.I. Baumgarten, and Alan Mendelson (Philadelphia: Fortress Press, 1981), 226–44, 391–403.

8. Chana Kronfeld, *On the Margins of Modernism: Decentering Literary Dynamics* (Berkeley: University of California Press, 1996), 28.

9. Albert I. Baumgarten, "Literary Evidence for Jewish Christianity in the Galilee," in *The Galilee in Late Antiquity*, ed. Lee I. Levine (New York: Jewish Theological Seminary of America, 1992), 39–50.

10. The era of the "Aryan Jesus" is over, thankfully. Susannah Heschel, *The Aryan Jesus: Christian Theologians and the Bible in Nazi Germany* (Princeton: Princeton University Press, 2008).

11. Craig C. Hill, "The Jerusalem Church," in *Jewish Christianity Reconsidered: Rethinking Ancient Groups and Texts*, ed. Matt Jackson-McCabe (Minneapolis: Fortress Press, 2007), 50.

1. From Son of God to Son of Man

1. Joseph Fitzmyer, *The One Who Is to Come* (Grand Rapids, MI: Eerdmans, 2007), 9. I have drawn much on Fitzmyer's exposition for this section.

2. To be sure, the person of the king has a sacralized quality, and moreover, as we see in the case of Saul himself, even an ecstatic or prophetic measure. (Is Saul among the prophets?)

3. For discussion, see A.Y. Collins and J.J. Collins, *King and Messiah as Son of God: Divine, Human, and Angelic Messianic Figures in Biblical and Related Literature* (Grand Rapids, MI: W.B. Eerdmans, 2008), 16–19.

4. Leo Baeck, *Judaism and Christianity: Essays* (Philadelphia: Jewish Publication Society of America, 1958), 28–29.

5. For a good survey, see Delbert Royce Burkett, *The Son of Man Debate: A History and Evaluation* (Cambridge: Cambridge University Press, 1999).

6. For the literature supporting this view, see John J. Collins, "The Son of Man and the Saints of the Most High in the Book of Daniel," *Journal of Biblical Literature* 93, no. 1 (March 1974):

50n2. In his view, the one like a son of man is Michael. He represents Israel, as its heavenly "prince," quite explicitly in chapters 10–12. Collins, accordingly, disagrees with me, thinking that the interpretation in Daniel 7 does not demote him at all. In both chapters 7 and 10–12, for Collins, reality is depicted on two levels. I would only remark that Collins's interpretation is by no means impossible, but I nonetheless prefer the one I have offered in the text for reasons made most clear in my article in the *Harvard Theological Review*, as well as on grounds of relative simplicity.

7. Louis Francis Hartman and Alexander A. Di Lella, *The Book of Daniel*, trans. Louis Francis Hartman, The Anchor Bible (Garden City, NY: Doubleday, 1978), 101. They themselves list Exod 13:21; 19:16; 20:21; Deut 5:22; I Kings 8:10; and Sir 45:4.

8. J.A. Emerton, "The Origin of the Son of Man Imagery," *Journal of Theological Studies* 9 (1958): 231–32.

9. Matthew Black, "The Throne-Theophany, Prophetic Commission, and the 'Son of Man,'" in *Jews, Greeks, and Christians: Religious Cultures in Late Antiquity: Essays in Honor of William David Davies*, ed. Robert G. Hamerton-Kelley and Robin Scroggs (Leiden: E.J. Brill, 1976), 61.

10. For a study of the ubiquity of this pattern, see Moshe Idel, *Ben: Sonship and Jewish Mysticism*, Kogod Library of Judaic Studies (London: Continuum, 2007).

11. Frank Moore Cross, *Canaanite Myth and Hebrew Epic* (Cambridge, MA: Harvard University Press, 1973), 43.

12. Readers of modern Hebrew will surely find Yisra'el Knohl, *Me-Ayin Banu: Ha-Tsofen Ha-Geneti Shel Ha-Tanakh* [The Genetic Code of the Bible] (Or Yehudah: Devir, 2008), 102–13, of interest here. Especially riveting is Knohl's idea that YHVH was represented by a golden calf insofar as he was understood as the son of El, who was a bull.

13. After the rabbis, I have found only Sigmund Olaf Plytt Mowinckel, *He That Cometh: The Messiah Concept in the Old Testament and Later Judaism*, trans. G.W. Anderson (Oxford: B. Blackwell, 1956), 352, emphasizing this point sufficiently, but, of course, since the literature is massive, I may (almost certainly have) missed others.

14. Following the argument made originally by Emerton, "Origin."

15. John J. Collins, *Daniel: A Commentary on the Book of Daniel*, Hermeneia (Minneapolis: Fortress Press, 1993), 291.

16. I have modified Collins's original list of such patterns in two ways. I have dropped the comparison with the sea, since I believe that the sea vision and the Son of Man vision were once two separate elements, and I have emphasized the differential ages of the two divine figures, which seems to me crucial for understanding the pattern of relationships here.

17. Carsten Colpe, "Ho Huios Tou Anthrōpou," in *Theological Dictionary of the New Testament*, vol. 8 (Grand Rapids, MI: Eerdmans, 1972), 8:400–477.

18. Ronald Hendel, "The Exodus in Biblical Memory," in *Remembering Abraham* (Oxford: Oxford University Press, 2005), 57–75.

19. Cross, *Canaanite*, 58. See also David Biale, "The God with Breasts: El Shaddai in the Bible," *History of Religions* 21, no. 3 (February 1982): 240–56, and Mark S. Smith, *The Early History of God: Yahweh and the Other Deities in Ancient Israel*, 2nd ed. with a foreword by Patrick D. Miller, Biblical Resources Series (Grand Rapids, MI: William B. Eerdmans, 2002), 184.

20. This explanation of Ba'al and YHVH as rivals for the young God spot might be taken to explain better the extreme rivalry between them manifested in the Bible.

21. Smith, *Early History of God*, 32–33. Cross, in contrast, had argued that YHVH was originally a cultic name for 'El used in the south; YHVH eventually splits off from and then ousts 'El (Cross, *Canaanite*, 71). This seems to me to leave somewhat unclear the Ba'al-like characteristic of YHVH as these have been described by Cross himself in the passage cited immediately above. Cross's comments (Cross, *Canaanite*, 75) on two strands in "Israel's primitive religion" don't quite answer this question. In a later chapter of his book, Cross treats the close affinities between Ba'al and YHVH, so close, indeed, that as my teacher H.L. Ginsberg realized already in the 1930s, an entire Ba'al hymn has been lifted intact and adapted for YHVH in Psalm 29. As Cross himself emphasizes, this could hardly have been done if the imagery were not appropriate already for YHVH (Cross, *Canaanite*, 156). Cross therefore writes:

"The language of theophany in early Israel was primarily language drawn from the theophany of Ba'l" (Cross, *Canaanite*, 157), a formulation that I would slightly modify: the language of theophany of YHVH in ancient Israel was parallel to and nearly identical to the language of theophanies of Ba'al among northern Canaanites. Cross, of course, recognizes the merger here, but it is less clear why, according to him, 'El/YHVH should have absorbed characteristics of Ba'al that seemingly did not exist before in Israel's religion. As Cross's reconstruction seems not to recognize YHVH as a variant of Ba'al, where would he come from? This difficulty is obviated if we assume an ancient cult of 'El as the universal old god of all of the Canaanites and Ba'al and YHVH as variant forms and names of the young god, with YHVH merged into 'El in the later forms of official biblical religion. Of course, I do not imagine for a second that YHVH did not further appropriate characteristics of Ba'al as he moved northward and became more of a rain and storm god in addition to the mountain and volcano god that he had been in his putative original southern home. See also Peter Hayman, "Monotheism—a Misused Word in Jewish Studies?" *Journal of Jewish Studies* 42, no. 1 (1991): 5. See also especially Paula Fredriksen, "Mandatory Retirement: Ideas in the Study of Christian Origins Whose Time Has Come to Go," in *Israel's God and Rebecca's Children: Christology and Community in Early Judaism and Christianity: Essays in Honor of Larry W. Hurtado and Alan F. Segal*, ed. David B. Capes et al. (Waco, TX: Baylor University Press, 2007), 35–38.

22. A similar explanation, mutatis mutandis, might, just might, help to understand the place of Ḥokhma, Lady Wisdom, as a virtual consort to God in Proverbs 8 and her connections with Ashera, for which see Smith, *Early History of God*, 133.

23. It is here that I part company most decisively with Otto Eissfeldt, "El and Yahweh," *Journal of Semitic Studies* 1 (1956): 25–37, and Margaret Barker, *The Great Angel: A Study of Israel's Second God* (London: SPCK, 1992).

24. Daniel Abrams, "The Boundaries of Divine Ontology: The Inclusion and Exclusion of Meṭaṭron in the Godhead," *Harvard Theological Review* 87, no. 3 (July 1994): 291–321.

25. *Pace* Barker, *Great Angel*, 40. I thus agree with Emerton's

conclusion that "the language used of the Son of man suggests Yahwe, not the Davidic king." Emerton, "The Origin," 231.

26. Seen in this light, it really is a sort of quibble to distinguish between second divinity and highest angel. We need to remember that in antiquity monotheism meant not the sole existence of only one divine being but the absolute supremacy of one to whom all others are subordinate (and this was good Christian theology until Nicaea as well). Fredriksen, "Mandatory Retirement," 35–38, is a concise, excellent presentation of this position.

27. "Yahoel" appears in the Apocalypse of Abraham (A.D. 70–150), but then as late as 3 Enoch (fourth–fifth centuries), we find "Little Yahu," "Yahoel Yah," and "Yahoel" explicitly given as names for Metatron. Andrei Orlov, "Praxis of the Voice: The Divine Name Traditions in the Apocalypse of Abraham," *Journal of Biblical Literature* 127 (2008): 53–70, and Philip S. Alexander, "The Historical Setting of the Hebrew Book of Enoch," *Journal of Jewish Studies* 28 (1977): 163–64. (See also in this context Gedaliahu G. Stroumsa, "Form[s] of God: Some Notes on Metatron and Christ: For Shlomo Pines," *Harvard Theological Review* 76, no. 3 [July 1983]: 269–88.) As Alexander points out in that article as well, these very names are predicated in other contemporary texts of God himself. The lines between exalted angels and gods get harder and harder to draw and see. "At some stage, the old myth was reinterpreted in terms of the supremacy of Yahwe, who had been identified with both Elyon and Baal. Then the Son of man was degraded to the status of an angel, even though he retained the imagery which was so closely attached to him in tradition. This would help to explain the attribution of an exalted status to such beings as Michael and Metatron in later Judaism" (Emerton, "The Origin," 242). It is important to add, however, that angel is not necessarily such a degradation, but perhaps precisely the point of a tension or ambiguity about monotheism at the heart of Israel's religion (this is more an explication of Emerton than a correction of him). Throughout the Hebrew Bible there is confusion between YHVH himself, as it were, and his Mal'akh, the single, unnamed angel of the Lord, precisely in theophanies. The first example of the use of the term in Genesis

already manifests this conflation. In Genesis 16:7 the "angel of YHVH" appears to Hagar and performs a series of clearly divine offices. No wonder that in v. 13, she refers to him as YHVH. As Robert Alter remarks in the name of Richard Elliot Friedman, "No clear-cut distinction between God and angel is intended." Similarly in Genesis 22:11–18, where clearly the angel of YHVH is performing precisely the offices of YHVH himself. Another brilliant example is Exodus 3, where Moses sees the angel of YHVH inside the burning bush and then in v. 7 the very same figure addresses him and is called YHVH. There is, indeed, no clear distinction between YHVH and this special Mal'akh; they are two aspects of one divinity but also the product of a productive tension derived from the hypothetic originary ditheism of Israel's religion.

28. Collins, *Daniel*, 281. Collins seems to consider the pattern of religion enshrined in the throne vision as a frozen relic from Israel's past (or even a foreign past): "it has been argued that motifs should not be 'torn out of their living contexts' but 'should be considered against the totality of the phenomenological conception of the works in which such correspondences occur.' Such demands are justified when the intention is to compare the 'patterns of religion' in a myth and a biblical text, but this has never been the issue in the discussion of Daniel 7."

29. See Daniel Boyarin, "Beyond Judaisms: Meṭaṭron and the Divine Polymorphy of Ancient Judaism," *Journal for the Study of Judaism in the Persian, Hellenistic, and Roman Periods* 41 (July 2010): 323–65.

30. Andrew Chester, "High Christology—Whence, When and Why?" *Early Christianity* 2, no. 1 (2011): 22–50.

31. Chester identifies three trends within the group of scholars who see the divinity of Christ as emerging within Jewry, defined almost according to the tempo of the emergence: (1) James Dunn's, according to which "high Christology emerges within essentially Jewish categories, but does so only very gradually," and it is in John that it emerges (in this respect like the first view but without necessitating Gentile sources); (2) Martin Hengel's and Larry Hurtado's, according to which high Christology emerges very rapidly—"explosively"—within

a Jewish context in response to the resurrection and is seen most clearly in Paul; and (3) the view of Horbury and Collins that I am maintaining here, namely, that the theological ideas behind a high Christology were already present within Second Temple Judaism. Chester, "High Christology," 31.

32. I have modified the translation of the end of the sentence (RSV: "but God alone") following Adela Yarbro Collins, *Mark: A Commentary*, ed. Harold W. Attridge, Hermeneia—a Critical and Historical Commentary on the Bible (Minneapolis: Fortress Press, 2007), 181, and see her discussion, 185.

33. Given the meaning of the underlying Aramaic word in Daniel, "authority" strikes me as a rather weak rendering; "sovereignty" would be much better. Sovereignty would surely explain why the Son of Man has the power to remit sins on earth.

34. Cf. Morna Hooker, *The Son of Man in Mark: A Study of the Background of the Term "Son of Man" and Its Use in St Mark's Gospel* (Montreal: McGill University Press, 1967), 90–91, who seems to take this (in partial contradiction to her own position earlier) to be significant of a prerogative of "man" in general.

35. This final insight was stimulated by a comment of Gudrun Guttenberger, followed by a further comment of Ishay Rosen-Zvi. See too Seyoon Kim, *"The 'Son of Man' " as the Son of God*, WUNT (Tübingen: J.C.B. Mohr, 1983), 2: "In claiming this divine prerogative Jesus classes himself as the Son of Man into the category of the divine, and his superhuman act of healing is the sign for this claim. So already in 1927 O. Procksch suggested that here 'the Son of Man' stands for the Son of God."

36. As New Testament scholar F.W. Beare has written, "In the gentile churches, this will not have been a burning question in itself; it will have arisen only as one aspect of the much broader issue of how far the Law of Moses was held to be binding upon Christians. Insofar as the pericope [discrete passage of the narrative] is a community-product, accordingly, it will be regarded as a product of Palestinian Jewish Christianity, not of the Hellenistic churches. The way to understanding will therefore lie through the examination of Jewish traditions and modes of thought." F.W. Beare, " 'The Sabbath Was Made for Man?' " *Journal of Biblical Literature* 79, no. 2 (June 1960): 130.

37. Generally, and this is highly important, New Testament critics have seen vv. 27–28 as an addition to an original text that incorporated only the answer regarding David—or the opposite, that only vv. 27–28 were original and that the reference to David is a secondary addition. "As Guelich observes (similarly Back, *Jesus of Nazareth*, 69; Doering, *Schabbat*, 409), these four suggestions basically boil down to two: (1) either Jesus' argument from the action of David is original, with vv. 27–28 being added later in one or two stages, or (2) v. 27 (and possibly v. 28) constituted Jesus' original answer(s), with the story of David being added later." John Paul Meier, "The Historical Jesus and the Plucking of the Grain on the Sabbath," *Catholic Biblical Quarterly* 66 (2004): 564.

38. Translation mine: ‏מכילתא דרבי ישמעאל כי תשא ˙ מסכתא דשבתא פרשה א.

39. To be sure, Matthew is frequently closer in thought and expression to rabbinic texts than Mark. It is this point, in fact, that has given rise to the notion that Matthew's Gospel is more "Jewish" than Mark's, a distinct error in my view, although Matthew may have been closer to proto-rabbinic traditions than Mark was. Rabbi Akiva's own argument is somewhat difficult to understand, but may be best understood as meaning something like this: We know that one removes a murderer from the altar, even in the midst of a sacrifice, from Exodus 21:14, where we are told of the premeditated murderer that "You shall take him from the altar to execute him." Now, it follows that redressing murder is more important than even the sacrifices, and the sacrifices are more important than the Sabbath (since the Sabbath is violated in the Temple in order to maintain the cult); therefore, argues Rabbi Akiva, it follows that saving a human life is more important than the Sabbath and sets it aside. The reasoning from executing the murderer to saving a life seems to be an instance of the general tannaitic principle that the measure of mercy is always more powerful than the measure of retribution. This will enable us to understand anew v. 6 there. When Jesus says, "I tell you, something greater than the temple is here," he is, at the first glance, simply anticipating the a fortiori argument that we hear later from Rabbi Akiva's mouth, to wit, that benefit to humans is greater than the worship in the Temple, and if, therefore, we violate

the Sabbath for the Temple worship, even more so for the benefit of humans. It must, however, also be recognized that Jesus'
halakhic statement is afforded a much more radical import in
that it includes a broader test for benefit, not merely the saving
of a life, as the Rabbis would have it, but also the saving from
hunger. (Cf. Aharon Shemesh, "Shabbat, Circumcision and
Circumcision on Shabbat in Jubilees and the Dead Sea Scrolls,"
unpublished paper [2011]. I am grateful to Prof. Shemesh for
his comments on this chapter and for sharing his work with
me prior to publication.) Finally, in a pattern that repeats itself
in Mark 7, as we shall see in chapter 3 below, Jesus' halakhic
argument—a virtually impeccable one and well formed on
rabbinic principles that are thus shown to be far older than the
Rabbis—is interpreted as a kind of parable and one with reference to the messianic age in which Jesus and the evangelist
were living. As Shemesh remarks, "It should be admitted that
in both arguments, Jesus makes a better case than the Rabbis."
40. Shemesh, "Shabbat."
41. There is a tendency among certain Christian scholars to in-
sist on an absolute contrast and hence conflict here between
"Judaism" (bad) and "Christianity" (good). Exemplary of this
tendency is Arland J. Hultgren, "The Formation of the Sabbath
Pericope in Mark 2:23–28," *Journal of Biblical Literature* 91,
no. 1 (March 1972): 39n8, who delivers himself of the following statement:

> There is a close parallel, to which many commentators
> refer, in the statement of the second century R. Simeon b.
> Menasya (Mekilta on Exod 31:14): "The sabbath is deliv-
> ered unto you, and you are not delivered to the sabbath."
> But this saying does not have the same meaning as Mark
> 2:27. In context it emphasizes the sabbath as a distinctive
> Jewish institution, i.e., as given to Israel (so Exod 31:14).
> The sabbath is delivered to Israel as a gift, and it is under-
> stood that Israel will therefore observe it. In Mark 2:27 it
> is understood that the sabbath has been established for
> man's good. It will be kept in a Jewish milieu, of course,
> but what is to prevail is that which enhances human life,
> not sabbath casuistry—even if the intention of the latter
> is to make the day one of celebration.

The willful ignorance displayed in this statement simply takes the breath away, since it is absolutely clear from the context that the saying of Rabbi Shim'on ben Menasya is, indeed, about the permission to heal on the Sabbath. Hultgren is precisely wrong; his sentence should read: "The Sabbath is delivered to Israel as a gift, and, therefore, it is permitted to heal Jews on Sabbath." Lest matters be less than clear, I emphasize that I am not denying the highly significant difference between Jesus and the Mekhilta (the Rabbis) here. The Rabbis surely restrict the permission to heal on the Sabbath to Jews, while Jesus seems to intend this to be a general permission to save all human life. It remains the case, nonetheless, that the Rabbis here use exactly the same argument to justify healing on the Sabbath as Jesus does, namely, that the Sabbath was given to human beings (Israel) for their welfare and that the humans were not given to the Sabbath. My point, then, is not to deny the possible moral superiority of Jesus' position over the Rabbis (see Shemesh in previous note) but to protest rather the assertion of absolute and total difference between allegedly polar opposite religious approaches, one allegedly rigid, harsh, and legalistic and the other promoting a humanistic religion of love. Hultgren's contemptuous use of "casuistry" gives his game away. Even more offensive than Hultgren's is the opinion of E. Lohse that "The Sabbath was made for man" etc. is an authentic saying of Jesus owing to its alleged *dissimilarity* from Judaism, following the highly questionable criterion that only what is not like "Judaism" can be asserted to be the actual words of the Lord. This statement is dissimilar from Judaism and therefore allegedly authentically dominical, since precisely the same statement when it does appear in Jewish texts (the Mekhilta, as above) "means something different." If there ever was an example of begging the question, this is it. The perversity of this kind of argument must be obvious, for even Occam's razor would demand that if we find the same (or virtually the same) saying in a similar context in two historically related texts, they must mean roughly the same thing. The special pleading involved in distorting the rabbinic saying from its obvious meaning in order to make it different (and "worse") than Jesus' and then using this as an implicit argument against "Judaism" is simply anti-Judaic special pleading. For the Lohse, see Frans Neirynck, "Jesus and the Sabbath: Some Observations on Mark Ii, 27," in *Jesus Aux Origines de la Christologie*, ed. J. Dupont et al., Bibliotheca Ephemeridum Theologicarum Lovaniensium (Louvain: Leuven University Press, 1975), 229–30. Neirynck himself surely gets this right; Neirynck, "Jesus and the Sabbath," 251–52. However, he is exactly wrong to say that "on both sides [i.e., with respect to the Gospel and the rabbinic saying] we are confronted with a variety of interpretations." No interpreter in the history of Judaism has ever seen this saying, nor does its context permit seeing it, as anything but a support for the principle that saving a life takes precedent over the Sabbath; any other readings by modern New Testament scholars are the product of prejudice and nothing else. The alleged "chaos of talmudic scholarship," at least in this instance, is a pure figment of the imagination. Much better is an interpreter such as William Lane, for whom the *similarity* of Jesus' saying to that of the Rabbis is taken as evidence in favor of its dominical origin (William L. Lane, *The Gospel According to Mark: The English Text with Introduction, Exposition, and Notes*, New International Commentary on the New Testament [Grand Rapids, MI: William B. Eerdmans, 1974], 119–20). More recent Christian scholars follow in this general tendency, such as Joel Marcus, *Mark 1–8: A New Translation with Introduction and Commentary* (New York: Doubleday, 2000), 245–46, and Collins, *Mark: A Commentary*, 203–4, who get this just right.

42. Menahem Kister, "Plucking on the Sabbath and the Jewish-Christian Controversy" [Hebrew], *Jerusalem Studies in Jewish Thought* 3, no. 3 (1984): 349–66. See also Shemesh, "Shabbat."

43. John P. Meier has written, "Clearly, then, this Galilean cycle of dispute stories is an intricate piece of literary art and artifice, written by a Christian theologian to advance his overall vision of Jesus as the hidden yet authoritative Messiah, Son of Man, and Son of God. As we begin to examine the fourth of the five stories, the plucking of the grain on the Sabbath, the last thing we should do is treat it like a videotaped replay of a debate among various Palestinian Jews in the year A.D. 28. It is, first of

all, a Christian composition promoting Christian theology. To what extent it may also preserve memories of an actual clash between the historical Jesus and Pharisees can be discerned only by analyzing the Christian text we have before us." Meier, "Plucking," 567. I completely agree with Meier's formulation here; the text will not allow us to see simplistically here only a record of halakhic controversies (although the fact that it allows us to see this *also* is of enormously precious importance). My dissent from Meier is only in his mobilization of the term "Christian" here as a term in opposition to "various Palestinian Jews." I would like to present here a reading based on my views expressed until now in which both the halakhic controversy and its apocalyptic radicality go back to the same Palestinian Jewish milieu.

44. The fact that David's action did not take place on the Sabbath is completely irrelevant, *pace* Meier, "Plucking," 576–77, and Collins, *Mark: A Commentary*, 203. Also partly disagreeing with Meier, I would suggest that Jesus' erroneous substitution of Abiatar for Ahimelek as the name of the high priest denotes familiarity with the biblical text, not ignorance, and rather supports the historicity of the moment. Someone very familiar with a text and quoting it from memory could easily make such a mistake, while a writer rarely would. I thus disagree on all points with the following sentence: "The conclusion we must draw both from this error and from the other examples of Jesus' inaccurate retelling of the OT story is simple and obvious: the recounting of the incident of David and Ahimelech shows both a glaring ignorance of what the OT text actually says and a striking inability to construct a convincing argument from the story;" Meier, "Plucking," 578. And I don't think I fall into the category of Meier's "conservative scholars." My reading, if he accepts it, could somewhat reduce Meier's "surprise" at discovering that Haenchen claims that the author (or inserter) of vv. 25–26 was knowledgeable in Scripture; Meier, "Plucking," 579n35., citing Ernst Haenchen, *Der Weg Jesu. Eine Erklärung Des Markus-Evangeliums und der Kanonischen Parallelen*, Sammlung Töpelmann, vol. 6. (Berlin: Töpelmann, 1966), 121. I believe that the Lukan version supports my interpretation in that the direct move from David to the Son of Man implies the

messianic parallelism strongly (Luke 6:4–5). For this reading of Luke, see Neirynck, "Jesus and the Sabbath," 230.

45. Cf. the similar but also subtly different conclusion of Collins, *Mark: A Commentary*, 205. For me, it is not so much the Messiah as king that is at issue but rather the Son of Man as carrier of divinity and divine authority on earth.

46. This interpretation obviates the apparent non sequitur between vv. 27 and 28, pointed to inter alia by Beare, " 'The Sabbath Was Made for Man?' " 130.

47. Cf. Robert H. Gundry, *Mark: A Commentary on His Apology for the Cross* (Grand Rapids, MI: Eerdmans, 2004 [1993]), I: 144. For other authors holding this view, see discussion in Neirynck, "Jesus and the Sabbath," 237–38, and notes there.

48. As far as I can tell, my view is closest in certain respects to that of Eduard Schweizer, *Das Evangelium Nach Markus* [Bible. 4, N.T. Mark. Commentaries], Das Neue Testament Deutsch (Gottingen: Vandenhoeck & Ruprecht, 1973), 39–40.

49. For discussion of these two apparent difficulties, see Marcus, *Mark 1–8*, 243–47.

50. This is, indeed, one of the main points of Shemesh's unpublished paper; indeed, Shemesh makes so (appropriately) bold as to argue that Jesus' halakhic arguments are not infrequently more coherent and cogent than some of those of the latter-day Rabbis. But they remain, none the less, and even more so, halakhic arguments.

51. Cf. Beare, " 'The Sabbath Was Made for Man?' " 134. I disagree with Beare, however, in his assumption that the David argument could only have been mobilized with messianic overtones, given that we find it in rabbinic literature without such overtones and in a very similar context, namely, as a justification for violating the Torah in a situation in which there is a threat to life (even a very mild such threat, such as a sore throat). Palestinian Talmud Yoma 8:6, 45:b.

52. For a similar view, see Collins, *Mark: A Commentary*, 185 n28.

2. The Son of Man in First Enoch and Fourth Ezra: Other Jewish Messiahs of the First Century

1. Howard Jacobson, *The Exagoge of Ezekiel* (Cambridge: Cambridge University Press, 1983), 55.

2. Richard Bauckham, "The Throne of God and the Worship of Jesus," in *The Jewish Roots of Christological Monotheism: Papers from the St. Andrews Conference on the Historical Origins of the Worship of Jesus*, ed. Carey C. Newman, Supplements to the Journal for the Study of Judaism (Boston: Brill, 1999), 53. See too Charles A. Gieschen, *Angelomorphic Christology: Antecedents and Early Evidence*, Arbeiten Zur Geschichte Des Antiken Judentums und Des Urchristentums (Leiden: Brill, 1998), 93–94.

3. For the formerly held position that the parables were earlier than this, see Matthew Black, "The Eschatology of the Similitudes of Enoch," *Journal of Theological Studies* 3 (1953): 1. For the latest and generally accepted position, see essays in Gabriele Boccaccini, ed., Jason von Ehrenkrook, assoc. ed., *Enoch and the Messiah Son of Man: Revisiting the Book of Parables* (Grand Rapids, MI: William B. Eerdmans, 2007), 415–98, especially David Suter, "Enoch in Sheol: Updating the Dating of the Parables of Enoch," 415–33.

4. "We certainly find blurring of the lines between human messiah and heavenly or angelic deliverer in the Son of Man tradition." Adela Yarbro Collins and John J. Collins, *King and Messiah as Son of God: Divine, Human, and Angelic Messianic Figures in Biblical and Related Literature* (Grand Rapids, MI: W.B. Eerdmans, 2008). It is of the Similitudes that the Collinses are speaking.

5. George W.E. Nickelsburg and James C. VanderKam, trans. and eds., *I Enoch: A New Translation* (Minneapolis: Fortress Press, 2004), 59–60.

6. It is not clear to me how the Aramaic עתיק יומן, something like "Ancient of Days," yields "head of days," but this is immaterial for the present case. For different solutions of this problem, see Matthew Black, in collaboration with James C. VanderKam and Otto Neugebauer, *The Book of Enoch, or Enoch: A New English Translation with Commentary and Textual Notes. With*

an Appendix on the "Astronomical" Chapters (72–82), SVTP (Leiden: E.J. Brill, 1985), 192.

7. The major exegetical work to demonstrate that this chapter is constructed as a midrash on Daniel 7:13–14 has been done by Lars Hartman, who shows carefully how many biblical verses and echoes there are in the chapter. Lars Hartman, *Prophecy Interrupted: The Formation of Some Jewish Apocalyptic Texts and of the Eschatological Discourse Mark 13*, Conjectanea Biblica (Stockholm: Almqvist and Wiksell, 1966), 118–26. My discussion in this and the next paragraph draws on his, so I will forgo a series of specific references. In any case, I can only summarize his detailed and impressive argument.

8. Pierluigi Piovanelli, " 'A Testimony for the Kings and Mighty Who Possess the Earth': The Thirst for Justice and Peace in the Parables of Enoch," in *Enoch and the Messiah Son of Man: Revisiting the Book of Parables*, ed. Gabriele Boccaccini (Grand Rapids, MI: Eerdmans, 2007).

9. Nickelsburg and VanderKam, *I Enoch: A New Translation*, 61–63.

10. Ibid., 91–92.

11. James R. Davila, "Of Methodology, Monotheism and Metatron," in *The Jewish Roots of Christological Monotheism: Papers from the St. Andrews Conference on the Historical Origins of the Worship of Jesus*, ed. Carey C. Newman, Supplements to the Journal for the Study of Judaism (Leiden: Brill, 1999), 9.

12. My reading here of the Similitudes is close to that of Morna Hooker, *The Son of Man in Mark: A Study of the Background of the Term "Son of Man" and Its Use in St Mark's Gospel* (Montreal: McGill University Press, 1967), 37–48.

13. Moshe Idel, *Ben: Sonship and Jewish Mysticism*, Kogod Library of Judaic Studies (London: Continuum, 2007), 4.

14. I am fully persuaded by the argument of Daniel Olson, "Enoch and the Son of Man," *Journal for the Study of the Pseudepigraphica* 18 (1998): 33, that chapter 70 also originally identified Enoch with the Son of Man. His article is exemplary philology in that it supports one variant of a manuscript tradition and then explains compellingly why that reading had been changed in other branches of the paradosis.

15. For a study of the ubiquity of this pattern, see Idel, *Ben*, 1–3.

16. Bauckham, "The Throne," 58.

17. Pierre Grelot, "La légende d'Hénoch dans les Apocryphes et dans la Bible: Origine et signification," *RSR* 46 (1958): 5–26, 181–220; James C. VanderKam, *Enoch and the Growth of an Apocalyptic Tradition* (Washington, DC: Catholic Biblical Association of America, 1984), 23–51; Helge S. Kvanvig, *Roots of Apocalyptic: The Mesopotamian Background of the Enoch Figure and of the Son of Man* (Neukirchen-Vluyn: Neukirchener Verlag, 1988), 191–213; Andrei A. Orlov, *The Enoch-Metatron Tradition*, Texte und Studien Zum Antiken Judentum (Tübingen: Mohr Siebeck, 2005), 23–78.

18. Kvanvig, *Roots*, 187; John J. Collins, "The Sage in Apocalyptic and Pseudepigraphic Literature," in *The Sage in Israel and the Ancient Near East*, ed. John G. Gammie (Winona Lake, IN: Eisenbrauns, 1990), 346.

19. Idel, *Ben*, 1–7. Earlier and more directly relating to such merger, see Moshe Idel, "Metatron: Notes Towards the Development of Myth in Judaism" [Hebrew], in *Eshel Beer-Sheva: Occasional Publications in Jewish Studies* (Beer-sheva: Ben-Gurion University of the Negev Press, 1996), 29–44.

20. Helge S. Kvanvig, "Henoch und der Menschensohn: Das Verhältnis von Hen 14 zu Dan 7," *ST* 38 (1984): 114–33.

21. This summary draws on Nickelsburg, *1 Enoch 1*, 255–56.

22. Black, VanderKam, and Neugebauer, *Enoch*, 151–52, accepts this position but offers as well the not implausible hypothesis of a common dependence on a work earlier than the two of these. In any case, this issue is immaterial for my investigation here.

23. Contrast Sigmund Olaf Plytt Mowinckel, *He That Cometh: The Messiah Concept in the Old Testament and Later Judaism*, trans. G. W. Anderson (Oxford: B. Blackwell, 1956), 384–85.

24. James Davila also reads the work of the so-called redactor (once again, I call him author) as having specific ideological/theological intent. Davila, "Of Methodology," 12. He doesn't interpret this activity in quite the way I do, however, but does note the very important point that the Hebrew 3 Enoch (and thus the Enoch-Metatron tradition) presupposes it.

25. Daniel Boyarin, "The Gospel of the Memra: Jewish Binitarianism and the Crucifixion of the Logos," *Harvard Theological*

Review 94, no. 3 (2001): 243–84. Note too Larry Hurtado's three categories of divine mediation: personified and hypostasized divine attributes, such as Wisdom or Logos; exalted patriarchs; and principal angels (Larry W. Hurtado, *One God, One Lord: Early Christian Devotion and Ancient Jewish Monotheism*, 2nd ed. [Edinburgh: T & T Clark, 1998]). To these James Davila adds two others, of which one seems relevant here: "archetypes based on earlier biblical characters and offices (e.g., the Davidic king, the Mosaic prophet, and the Aaronid high priest) but whose incarnation as individuals is projected either into the future (future ideal figures) or into the heavenly realm (exalted ideal figures)." Davila, "Of Methodology," 6.

26. Bauckham, "The Throne," 61.

27. I find incomprehensible, therefore, Baukham's claim that "early Christians said about Jesus what no other Jews had wished to say about the Messiah or any other figure; that he had been exalted by God to participate now in the cosmic sovereignty unique to the divine identity" (Bauckham, "The Throne," 63), since Bauckham himself had just demonstrated the significance of Enoch in this regard. To answer, as he does implicitly in the next paragraph, that "the Parables represent a parallel rather than a source" does not in any way impugn the authority of the Similitudes to render his claim false; in fact, as I have argued here, it enhances it, since now we have at least two independent witnesses to this religious concept, neither dependent on the other. Further, it should be emphasized that accepting Bauckham's premise, which seems compelling, that there are not a series of semi-divine mediator figures within Second Temple Judaism to which Jesus could have been assimilated forces us to recognize that Daniel 7:13–14 already assumes that the Son of Man shares in God's divinity, thus once again giving the lie to Bauckham's claim to some absolute uniqueness to Christology in the Jesus version. The Similitudes and the Gospels represent two developments out of the Danielic tradition. Of course, this does not preclude further religious creativity on the part of each of these traditions, as we see from the Gospels' apparent powerful addition of Psalm 110:1 to the mix (if Bauckham is right) and the continuation of the Enoch tradition in 3 Enoch (if he is, as I suppose, wrong).

28. Michael Edward Stone, *Fourth Ezra: A Commentary on the Book of Fourth Ezra*, ed. Frank Moore Cross, Hermeneia—a Critical and Historical Commentary on the Bible (Minneapolis: Fortress Press, 1990), 381–82.

29. Ibid., 383.

30. Ibid., 387.

31. I offer a different way of approaching the Son of Man, an approach that doesn't so much resolve the famous Son of Man debate but makes an end run around it by asking different questions. Joel Marcus has made this same point in quite another language when he wrote, "This conclusion [that the "Son of Man" in the Similitudes is pre-Christian] is supported by the way in which Jesus, in the Gospels, generally treats the Son of Man as a known quantity, never bothering to explain the term, and the way in which certain of this figure's characteristics, such as his identity with the Messiah or his prerogative of judging, are taken for granted. With apologies to Voltaire, we may say that if the Enochic Son of Man had not existed, it would have been necessary to invent him to explain the Son of Man sayings in the Gospels." Joel Marcus, *Mark 1–8: A New Translation with Introduction and Commentary* (New York: Doubleday, 2000), 530.

32. Carsten Colpe, "Ho Huios Tou Anthrōpou," in *Theological Dictionary of the New Testament* (Grand Rapids, MI: Eerdmans, 1972), 8:420.

3. Jesus Kept Kosher

1. This is partly dependent on the very common view that Mark himself, the author of the Gospel of Mark, was a believer from the Gentiles for whom the practices of eating kosher were entirely foreign and off-putting. The consequence of these two positions when put together is that at its earliest moment, the Jesus movement was characterized by a total shift in ideas about how to serve God, becoming entirely other to Judaism. The other evangelists, especially Matthew, who openly portray a Jesus who is much more friendly toward the Torah as practice, are understood as the product of communities referred

to by names such as Jewish-Christian or Judaizing communities, themselves terms of art in an ancient Christian discourse about heresy.

2. Adela Yarbro Collins, *Mark: A Commentary*, ed. Harold W. Attridge, Hermeneia—a Critical and Historical Commentary on the Bible (Minneapolis: Fortress Press, 2007), 356. It should be emphasized that Collins does not consider this necessarily the meaning of Jesus' original pronouncement at v. 15, but she does so read v. 19, which is a gloss by the evangelist Mark, thus rendering Mark (like Paul) the beginning of the end of the Law for Christians.

3. Robert A. Guelich, *Mark 1–8:26*, Word Biblical Commentary 34A; Mark; I–VIII (Dallas, TX: Word Books, 1989), 380.

4. Joel Marcus, *Mark 1–8: A New Translation with Introduction and Commentary* (New York: Doubleday, 2000), 450. It should be noted clearly, lest there be anything misleading here, that Marcus does consider Mark a "Jewish Christian," albeit a much more radical one than Matthew (more on this below in this chapter).

5. See too for instance, "Mark, our earliest gospel, offers a more reliable standard [than Paul]; and it says that Jesus abrogated laws of food and purity and violated the Sabbath"; Robert H. Gundry, *Mark: A Commentary on His Apology for the Cross* (Grand Rapids, MI: Eerdmans, 1993, 2004). This may be "a known fact" for Gundry; hardly for me.

6. See different translation here offered below.

7. Substituting the literal "curses" for the NRSV's "speaks evil of." I may be able to suggest a solution to a hermeneutic problem here. Marcus writes: "But, wrong as it may be to withhold material support from one's parents, how is it equivalent to *cursing* them?" (Marcus, *Mark 1–8*, 444) If we think of the Hebrew, however, this is perhaps less of a problem. In Hebrew the verb for "to honor" is literally to "make heavy," perhaps something like "to treat with gravitas." On the other hand, the word for "curse" is to "make light." So in Exodus 20, the verse reads, literally, "Make heavy your father and your mother," while in 21:17 it reads, "All who make light their father and mother shall surely die." If to make heavy (to honor) is to provide with material support, then to make light (to curse) is the opposite,

so not feeding one's parents is tantamount to cursing them. If this interpretation is appealing, then it would be evidence for at least a stratum in Mark that was much closer to the *veritas Hebraicas.*

8. Following Martin Goodman, who writes, "Jesus (or Matthew) was attacking Pharisees for their eagerness in trying to persuade other Jews to follow Pharisaic *halakah*"; Martin Goodman, *Mission and Conversion: Proselytizing in the Religious History of the Roman Empire* (Oxford: Clarendon Press, 1994), 70. This is surely not the only possible interpretation, but it is the one that makes the most sense to me.

9. To be sure, the confusion has been partly engendered by the biblical usage itself. There is one area in which the terminology is muddled. Of the animals that we may eat and may not eat, the Torah uses the terms "pure" and "impure." Nonetheless, the distinction between the two systems—what makes foods kosher or not and what makes kosher foods impure or not—remains quite clear despite this terminological glitch. In the later tradition, only the word "kosher" is used for the first, while "pure" means only undefiled.

10. These words usually translated "and all the Jews" make no sense according to that usual translation, as they almost directly contradict the point of the whole pericope. Why attack the Pharisees alone if their practice is simply the practice of all the Jews? For "Judeans" as one legitimate translation of *Ioudaioi,* if not the only one always and everywhere, see most recently Steve Mason, "Jews, Judaeans, Judaizing, Judaism: Problems of Categorization in Ancient History," *Journal for the Study of Judaism* 38, nos. 4–5 (2007): 457–512. It should be noted also that the translation "Judaeans" rather than "Jews" obviates comments that suggest that Mark by writing this is indicating a position outside of Jewry. Cf. Guelich, *Mark 1–8: 26,* 364.

11. Marcus, *Mark 1–8,* 439, but on 441 he is still doubtful. I, of course, agree with the translation, disagree with the doubt.

12. See also Stephen M. Reynolds, "Πυγμῇ (Mark 7:3) as 'Cupped Hand,'" *Journal of Biblical Literature* 85, no. 1 (March 1966): 87–88, supported by the late great talmudic scholar Saul Lieberman, my teacher (in a letter to Reynolds): "The custom of

shaping the hands like cups when they were washed for ritual purposes from a vessel was most probably very old. The opening of the [vessel] was usually not a large one; water in Palestine was valuable. When one forms the hand like a loose fist the narrow stream of water covers at once the entire outer and inner surfaces of the hand. Water is saved in this way. For purposes of cleanliness it was sufficient to pour some water on part of the hand, which could subsequently be spread all over the hand by rubbing both hands. Pouring water on 'cupped hands' immediately indicated ritual washing in preparation for a meal." Unfortunately, this highly attractive and significant interpretation had been almost totally ignored until just the last two decades or so, despite its being obviously correct in my opinion. Cf., for instance, "Standaert (Marc, 472–73) also repeats Hengel's argument from an earlier work ('Mk 7,3 Πυγμῇ: die Geschichte einer exegetische Aporie und der Versuch ihrer Losung,' ZNW 60 [1969] 182–98) that πυγμῇ in Mark 7:3 is a Latinism, but the derivation and meaning of πυγμῇ are so obscure that no firm conclusions can be drawn about it (cf. Guelich, *Mark 1–8:26*, 364–65), 16"; Joel Marcus, "The Jewish War and the Sitz Im Leben of Mark," *Journal of Biblical Literature* 111, no. 3 (1992): 444n15. Many scholars, especially Europeans, seem still to hold that Mark must be a Gentile, in part owing to his alleged ignorance of Jewish practice. I hope that this book will at least unsettle this view some.

13. The hermeneutic logic here is similar to that of Marcus in re Mark 2:23 (Marcus, *Mark 1–8*, 239) where the emphasis on "making a way" is taken as an allusion to the way that Jesus is making in the wilderness (the field). I am suggesting that Mark's emphasis on "with a fist," which is in itself quite realistic but seemingly trivial, has a similar symbolic overtone.

14. Yair Furstenberg, "Defilement Penetrating the Body: A New Understanding of Contamination in Mark 7.15," *New Testament Studies* 54 (2008): 178.

15. Tomson, 81, has brought this text to bear on Mark 7. It should be further pointed out, according to the Babylonian Talmud Shabbat 14a, that Rabbi Eliezer holds an even stricter standard than this; it is still within the category of rabbinic

(Pharisaic) innovation or the "traditions of the Elders," just as Jesus dubs it.

16. Furstenberg, "Defilement," 200.
17. Collins, *Mark: A Commentary*, 350. Given, however, that she so precisely articulates this, I cannot understand how on the next page she approves of Claude Montefiore's statement that "the argument in vv. 6–8 is not compelling." It is as compelling as can be as described above: "Why, Pharisees, are you setting aside the commandments of God in favor of the commandments of humans—handwashings, vows—as the Prophet prophesied?"
18. *Pace* Collins, *Mark: A Commentary*, 356.
19. Marcus, *Mark 1–8*, 444.
20. In chapter 2, there is also a passage that is, I think, illuminated by such a perspective. In vv. 18–22, some people wonder why other pietists (the disciples of John and the Pharisees) engage in fasting practices, while the disciples of Jesus do not. Jesus answers that they may not fast in the presence of the bridegroom, which is clearly a *halakhic* statement interpreted spiritually to refer to the holy, divine Bridegroom of Israel. As Yarbro Collins makes clear, this is another indirect claim on Jesus' part to be divine (*Mark: A Commentary*, 199).
21. "It seems that this is not the only occasion on which Jesus defends a conservative halakhic stand. In the woe-sayings in Matt 23, Jesus twice rails against Pharisaic law and offers an alternative halakhic opinion. In both matters, that of oaths (vv. 16–22) and the subject of purifying vessels (vv. 25–26), Jesus objects to the leniency of the Pharisees and offers a stricter ruling. This point is stressed by K.C.G. Newport, *The Sources and Sitz im Leben of Matthew 23* (JSNTSup 117; Sheffield: Sheffield Academic Press, 1995), 137–45" (Furstenberg, "Defilement," 178).
22. Albert I. Baumgarten, "The Pharisaic *Paradosis*," *Harvard Theological Review* 80 (1987): 63–77.
23. This is close to the view of Seán Freyne, *Galilee, from Alexander the Great to Hadrian, 323 B.C.E. to 135 C.E.: A Study of Second Temple Judaism*, University of Notre Dame Center for the Study of Judaism and Christianity in Antiquity, 5 (Wilmington, DE: M. Glazier, 1980), 316–18, 322.

24. Seeing Mark this way thoroughly reorients our understanding of its relation to the Gospel of Matthew as well. Let's look at the crucial parallel text from Matthew 15:

> [15]But Peter said to him, "Explain the parable to us." [16]Then he said, "Are you also still without understanding? [17]Do you not see that whatever goes into the mouth enters the stomach, and goes out into the sewer? [18]But what comes out of the mouth proceeds from the heart, and this is what defiles. [19]For out of the heart come evil intentions, murder, adultery, fornication, theft, false witness, slander. [20]These are what defile a person, but to eat with unwashed hands does not defile."

The Matthean text makes explicit that which might be ambiguous in Mark as we've read it. From beginning to end of the passage, it's not about anything but washing of the hands. There is not the slightest suggestion in Matthew that Jesus abrogated the laws of permitted and forbidden foods: Matthew's Jesus certainly kept kosher, a fact that no one can deny. But is Matthew a "Judaizing" revision of Mark, as many commentators have it, one who backed off from the radical implications of Mark's Jesus? Is it genuine, "original" Christian orthodoxy to hold that the kosher laws written in Moses' Torah mean nothing (and by implication all of the other so-called ritual laws of the Torah), with Matthew a temporizing voice that actually serves to neutralize the authentic Christian message on the Law as represented by Mark and Paul, namely, that Christianity is a whole new religion, an entirely different way of serving God from the way that the Israelites and Jews have understood it? On my reading, it is not. Whether Mark comes first (as I believe) or Matthew comes first (as a few scholars still hold), either way Jesus kept kosher and thus was kept kosher. Torah-abiding Jesus folks are not aberrant; they simply are the earliest Church.

25. Weston La Barre, *The Ghost Dance: Origins of Religion* (London: Allen and Unwin, 1972), 254.

4. The Suffering Christ as a Midrash on Daniel

1. Joseph Klausner, "The Jewish and Christian Messiah," in *The Messianic Idea in Israel, from Its Beginning to the Completion of the Mishnah*, trans. W.F. Stinespring (New York: Macmillan, 1955), 519–31.
2. Ibid., 526.
3. Ibid., 526–27.
4. See Martin Hengel, "The Effective History of Isaiah 53 in the Pre-Christian Period," in *The Suffering Servant: Isaiah 53 in Jewish and Christian Sources*, ed. Bernd Janowski and Peter Stuhlmacher, trans. Daniel P. Bailey (Grand Rapids, MI: William B. Eerdmans, 2004), 137–45, for good arguments to this effect. Hengel concludes, *"The expectation of an eschatological suffering savior figure connected with Isaiah 53 cannot therefore be proven to exist with absolute certainty and in a clearly outlined form in pre-Christian Judaism.* Nevertheless, a lot of indices that must be taken seriously in texts of very different provenance suggest that these types of expectations could *also* have existed at the margins, next to many others. This would then explain how a suffering or dying Messiah surfaces in various forms with the Tannaim of the second century C.E., and why Isaiah 53 is clearly interpreted messianically in the Targum and rabbinic texts" (140). While there are some points in Hengel's statement that require revision, the Targum is more a counterexample than a supporting text, and for the most part he is spot on.
5. Hengel, "Effective History," 133–37, even makes a case that the Septuagint (Jewish Greek translation) to Isaiah (second century B.C.) may already have read the Isaiah passage as referring to the Messiah.
6. While it is universally acknowledged that vv. 14:61–64 are an unambiguous allusion to Daniel 7:13, scholars who cannot abide the idea that Jesus himself claimed messianic status or to be the Son of Man have either denied that these could have been Jesus' true words (Lindars) or understood them as Jesus speaking about someone else (Bultmann) (and see 13:25 as well). The clear sense of these words, however, as written by Mark in his Gospel is that here Jesus speaks of himself.

7. See the absolutely convincing Joel Marcus, "Mark 14:61: 'Are You the Messiah-Son-of-God?' " *Novum Testamentum* 31, no. 2 (April 1989): 139. Incidentally, the comparison between this passage and 8:31 demonstrates that Jesus answers questions about his Messiahship by using the term "Son of Man," which is accordingly equivalent to Messiah in extension. He uses the term "Son of Man" in these instances because he is crucially calling up in both cases the Danielic context. This obviates the problem seen by some commentators to the effect that Jesus does not answer Peter affirmatively when Peter confesses him the Messiah. See Morna Hooker, *The Son of Man in Mark: A Study of the Background of the Term "Son of Man" and Its Use in St Mark's Gospel* (Montreal: McGill University Press, 1967), 104–5. Hooker herself suggests a similar interpretation to mine on 112; see 126 as well.

8. See Hooker, *Son of Man in Mark*, 118–19, for a related reconstruction, and especially 120–22.

9. C.H. Dodd, *According to the Scriptures: The Sub-Structure of New Testament Theology* (London: Nisbet, 1952), 116–19. Dodd ascribed the transfer of this theme from the People of the Holy Ones of God (a corporate entity) to Jesus (an individual) on the basis of an alleged "Christian exegetical tradition which thinks of Jesus as the inclusive representative of the People of God." The "Christian" exegetical tradition has its point of origin in Daniel 7, which was then naturally joined in the manner of midrash with the suffering servant of Isaiah 53 and to the Psalms of the Righteous Sufferer, for which there was apparently also a tradition of messianic reading. I think, however, that this is not a special Christian exegetical tradition but one that is plausible enough to have been the extant Jewish tradition even aside from Jesus.

10. I do not know early evidence outside of the Gospels for this particular way of reading the Daniel material as applying to a suffering Messiah, still less to a dying and rising one, and I have no reason to think that it did not fall into place in this particular Jewish Messianic movement. (As we shall see below, however, the reading of this as referring to the Messiah is not unknown to later rabbinic Judaism, not at all.) It should be noted that also in Fourth Ezra, discussed above in chapter 2, an

enemy arises to the Messiah, an enemy eventually defeated by him forever and ever.

11. This punctuation is Wellhausen's, as reported in Joel Marcus, *The Way of the Lord: Christological Exegesis of the Old Testament in the Gospel of Mark* (Louisville, KY: Westminster/John Knox Press, 1992), 99.

12. Ibid., 97.

13. Ibid., 100.

14. Marcus's great insight was that the Gospel text thematizes the contradiction. He somewhat goes off track in the beginning of his discussion by citing (in the way of Dahl) the tannaitic rule of "two verses that contradict each other"; the correct comparison is to the midrashic form of the Mekhilta, which is given later. This initial confusion has some consequences, for which see below.

15. From here on, I will be following Marcus quite closely. Marcus, *Way of the Lord*, 106.

16. It should be noted that in some respects the Matthean parallel goes in quite a different direction from Mark, especially by leaving out the crucial "It is written" statements in both instances. There is no midrash in Matthew here at all. For other entailed differences in this passage between the second and the first Gospels, see W.D. Davies and Dale C. Allison Jr., *A Critical and Exegetical Commentary on the Gospel According to Saint Matthew*, International Critical Commentary (Edinburgh: T & T Clark, 1988), 712. If Marcus and I are right, then Mark is much closer to a Jewish hermeneutical form than Matthew at this point.

17. Marcus, *Way of the Lord*, 108. Truth be told, in tannaitic literature much more often the first, but there are examples of the latter pattern as well in which the suggested interpretation is rejected. To my mind, saying "as it has been written" of the Son of Man that he will suffer is an entirely plausible scriptural inference. Marcus is still a bit misled by his confusion of two separate midrashic forms: (1) two verses that contradict each other and must be reconciled, and (2) a verse that contradicts the implication of an interpretive move that then can be refuted (as in the passages from the Mekhilta that Marcus correctly cites). It is only owing to this conflation that Marcus can

claim that "a hermeneutical rule for the treatment of a biblical text is here applied to a Christian midrash." It is, moreover, the midrash of the scribes that is refuted here by Jesus. It is a virtue of Marcus's reading, as amended here, that it obviates the need to ascribe ineptitude to Mark (cf. Davies and Allison, *Critical*, 710). The point nonetheless stands that Mark's text is a *lectio dificilior* here.

18. Origen, *Contra Celsum*, trans. with an introduction and notes by Henry Chadwick (Cambridge: Cambridge University Press, 1965), 50.

19. This version is almost certainly anterior to the Babylonian Talmud's parallel, which indicates that it is the Messiah, Son of Joseph, for whom they are mourning. This alternative Messiah, known only from the Babylonian Talmud and later texts, seems precisely to represent a sort of apologetic way of avoiding the implications of earlier traditions within which the Messiah suffers and/or is slain, such as is clear from the PT version of this tradition. David C. Mitchell, "Rabbi Dosa and the Rabbis Differ: Messiah Ben Joseph in the Babylonian Talmud," *Review of Rabbinic Judaism* 8, no. 1 (2005): 77–90, could hardly be more wrong in his interpretation of the rabbinic material. He insists that the Palestinian Talmudic text is tannaitic, notwithstanding the fact that it says "two Amoraim" explicitly; he considers the Babylonian Talmudic text primary and the Palestinian one secondary, and he seems to think that if the saying is quoted in the name of Rabbi Dosa, that means that it is something that actually was said by a figure who lived while the Temple still stood. Finally, he insists that a text cited explicitly as amoraic must be tannaitic simply because its diction is Hebrew and all Hebrew texts, *eo ipso*, are Palestinian and before A.D. 200, which further reveals his innocence of rabbinic textual knowledge. I know of no evidence for a Messiah the son of Joseph before late antiquity. Claims to find one in the Hazon Gabriel of the first century B.C. seem highly suspect since this finding would be dependent on a very doubtful reading indeed. Israel Knohl, "The Apocalyptic and Messianic Dimensions of the Gabriel Revelation in Their Historical Context," *Hazon Gabriel: New Readings of the Gabriel Revelation*, ed. Matthias Henze, Early Judaism and Its Literature, 29 (Atlanta: Society

of Biblical Literature, 2011), 43, may perhaps be correct in reading the name Ephraim in ll. 16–17 of this newly discovered text, but the reading is at best doubtful and in the opinion of some expert epigraphers impossible. See Elisha Qimron and Alexey Yuditsky, "Notes on the So-Called Gabriel Vision Inscription," *Hazon Gabriel: New Readings of the Gabriel Revelation*, ed. Matthias Henze, Early Judaism and Its Literature, 29 (Atlanta: Society of Biblical Literature, 2011), 34. It seems rather a weak read [*sic*] on which to base a second Messiah nearly half a millennium before its attestation in the literature. See also papers of Adela Yarbro Collins and John J. Collins in same volume for further corroboration of this position. If the Palestinian Talmud, then, imagines a dead Messiah, it must be *the* Messiah and not a second or other Messiah of which it speaks. Note that the supposed existence of a "War Messiah" in rabbinic literature is a chimera. "The one anointed—*mashuah* not *mashiah*—for war" is a special priest and nothing else, as an examination of every place in rabbinic literature where the term occurs confirms easily. Holger Zellentin's interpretation of the Babylonian Talmudic passage may have some merit in finding an allusion to Christian passion narratives there, but his claim that it is based on an earlier narrative of a double Messiah seems shaky in the extreme to me; Holger Zellentin, "Rabbinizing Jesus, Christianizing the Son of David: The Bavli's Approach to the Secondary Messiah Traditions," in *Discussing Cultural Influences: Text, Context and Non-Text in Rabbinic Judaism*, ed. Rivka Ulmer, Studies in Judaism (Lanham, MD: University Press of America, 2007), 99–127. To be sure, the BT does not seem to be inventing the concept here; rather, it is reflecting a known entity, but one for whom there is no prior evidence whatever within any extant text. When the Palestinian Talmud says that the Messiah died, therefore, it can only mean *the* Messiah.

20. The word for "disease" here means "leprosy" throughout rabbinic literature and is translated *leprosus* by Jerome as well (for the latter reference, see Adolph Neubauer, *The Fifty-Third Chapter of Isaiah According to the Jewish Interpreters* (Oxford: J. Parker, 1876–1877), 6.

21. But since it is only known from a volume of polemic Testimonia

(of a thirteenth-century Dominican friar), it might be considered suspect. See next note.

22. Raymondo Martini, *Pugio Fidei, Cum Observationibus Josephi de Voisin, et Introductione J. B. Carpzovj, Qui Appendicis Loco Hermanni Judœi Opusculum De Sua Conversion Ex Mscto . . . Recensuit* (Lipsiae, 1687), 674. Martini cites this text as from the fourth-century Midrash Siphre. I don't know if that citation is accurate, and one must question whether this is a real rabbinic text. On the other hand, although Martini was a polemicist, even his considerable powers as a Hebraist would not seem to have permitted him to forge a text in such fine midrashic style. Modern Jewish scholars from Leopold Zunz to my own teacher Saul Lieberman have accepted Martini's testimoniae as authentic texts.

23. Neubauer, *Fifty-Third Chapter*, 23.

24. Ibid., 258.

25. Ibid., 78.

26. I am not claiming that therefore the followers of Jesus did not originate this particular midrash, rather, if and when they did so, the hermeneutical practice they were engaged in bespoke in itself the "Jewishness" of their religious thinking and imagination.

27. Martin Hengel, "Christianity as a Jewish-Messianic Movement," in *The Beginnings of Christianity: A Collection of Articles*, ed. Jack Pastor and Menachem Mor (Jerusalem: Yad Ben-Zvi Press, 2005), 85, emphasis in original.

Epilogue

1. Adela Yarbro Collins, "Response to Israel Knohl, Messiahs and Resurrection in 'The Gabriel Revelation,' " in *Hazon Gabriel: New Readings of the Gabriel Revelation*, ed. Matthias Henze, Early Judaism and Its Literature, 29 (Atlanta: Society of Biblical Literature, 2011), 97.

Index